WAY

Christmas Ideas for Families

Phyllis Pellman Good
and
Merle Good

Good Books

Intercourse, PA 17534

The recipes for Injera, Wat, and Lemon Loaf
are reprinted by permission of Herald Press, Scottdale, PA
from *Extending the Table* by Joetta Handrich Schlabach.

Cover artwork and illustrations by Cheryl Benner
Design by Dawn J. Ranck

CHRISTMAS IDEAS FOR FAMILIES
Copyright © 1995 by Good Books, Intercourse, PA 17534
International Standard Book Number: 1-56148-180-7
Library of Congress Card Catalog Number: 95-44299

Library of Congress Cataloging-in-Publication Data

Good, Phyllis Pellman, 1948-
    Christmas ideas for families / Phyllis Pellman Good and Merle
Good.
        p. cm.
    ISBN 1-56148-180-7
    1. Christmas--United States. 2. Family recreation--United States.
3. United States--Social life and customs. I. Good, Merle, 1946-. II. Title
GT4986.A1G68   1995
394.2'663'0973--dc20   95-44299
                                                          CIP

Table of Contents

Introduction

The hundreds of ideas in this book are not just based on theory—they come from actual experience!

We invited families from a variety of settings to share with us their best ideas and experiences related to the many aspects of Christmas.

Because these pages come from real lives rather than from a theoretical workbook, we've tried to retain as much of the tone and quality of each family as possible. So don't be surprised to find a reference to food in the middle of some great decorating ideas. We believe the voice of each family's experience is as important to you, the reader, as is a mere list of ideas.

We hope you enjoy this collection as much as we have. Best wishes in creating new traditions and memories with your family and with others beyond your family!

—Phyllis Pellman Good and Merle Good

I.

Decorating Ideas and Traditions

★ Each year our family chooses a Christmas theme. We center our decorations and celebrations around the theme.

One year we chose *The Nutcracker Suite*—we went to hear *The Nutcracker Suite*, we did a puzzle together on nutcrackers, we went to the library and got books on nutcrackers.

Sometimes we pick a country (for example, Austria), learn about the country, and make decorations and food from that country.

This year our theme was "gifts." We decorated inside and out with empty boxes wrapped in Christmas paper. Our activities centered around gifts of ourselves to others. We volunteered as a family at the local nursing home, we invited friends into our home for simple meals throughout December, and we delivered a food package to a needy family.

—*Dennis, Sharon, Daniel, and Heather Showalter*
West Liberty, OH

★ The annual "gathering of the greens" and diligently searching for the "perfect" tree on our mountain property is an annual tradition for us. We gather large bags of Scotch pine, white pine, and fir. We use these greens and many treasures we find in our own backyard—holly, rhododendron, berries, pinecones, sweet gum and fox wood—to create wreaths and sprays for family and friends. Fresh greens also adorn our windowsills.

Trimming the house and tree is a really special family time for us, with Christmas music to set the mood. We all work together and enjoy "discovering" our favorite ornaments each year. (Nearly all of our ornaments were given to us by friends or family.) The evening ends with warm drinks by the newly lighted tree, and someone exclaiming, "It's the prettiest one ever!"

—Dale, Stephanie, Ashley, and Zachary Kaufman
Strasburg, PA

★ For most of my childhood years, we didn't have a Christmas tree that we bought specifically for the season. We often decorated a small pine that kept growing inside all year long. Now, although I enjoy Christmas trees, I also like to find alternatives, such as putting white lights on a fig tree or on top of the piano. I use a lot of natural lights such as oil lamps

and candles to provide atmosphere as well. This year I found a book of origami in the library and used wrapping paper to create all kinds of new decorations.

—Elaine Shenk, Elkhart, IN

★ We have several nativity sets. One I made from material printed with the nativity characters. I cut them out, sewed them up, and stuffed them. There is also a stable included in it. The grandchildren can play with it any time they want to while we tell them the real Christmas story.

Another one is a wooden puzzle nativity set made by my husband. It has all the different pieces: Mary, Joseph, shepherds, wise men, sheep, cattle, camels, and manger. The frame of the puzzle is the stable. This can either be set up or played with by children.

One year we bought a live blue spruce Christmas tree, planted it in a tub, and decorated it. After Christmas we planted it in our yard in the hole we dug before the ground froze. Today we have a beautiful, large, spruce tree growing in our yard.

—Marjora Miller, Archbold, OH

★ A part of our family holiday tradition has been the decorating of our own handbuilt contemporary stainless steel tree. It has many partly hidden enclosures where colorful miniature items may be placed and "discovered" by the viewers. Family and friends contribute to the uniqueness of the symbols each year.

Sometimes we cut hedge apples into thin slices, bake them in the kitchen oven to a desired color, and then hang them on the tree. The simple loveliness of the hedge apple is a welcome contrast to the commercial pressures of Christmas.

—Cornelia and Arlie J. Regier
Overland Park, KS

★ When our children were small, we solved the problem of them re-decorating our tree every day—we cut small branches from the large cedar trees in our yard and placed them in a Crisco can filled with gravel. Our children were each given an odd assortment of decorations—they were allowed to decorate their "trees," which we placed in their bedrooms, any way they wished. As they grew older, we let them put lights on their branches. They spent a lot of time in their rooms, watching their "trees."
— *Faye and Harry Pankratz, Inola, OR*

> *"Last year our five-year-old*
> *hung her ornaments*
> *in one clump on the tree,*
> *and I had to practice great self-control*
> *not to spread them out."*

★ I have boxed up our Christmas decorations in smaller boxes, labeled by room or content. Beginning the first week of December, we unpack only one or two boxes each week. One day we decorate the children's bedrooms, another day we decorate one of our two trees, and another day we decorate the exterior of our home.

We try not to rush the day's project and to involve the children as much as possible. This reduces the stress of trying to locate all of the decorations for one room that may be spread out in several boxes. It also involves the entire family.

We try to purchase or make one ornament each year that will remind us of a special event which took place that year. Our children also receive ornaments from their grandparents each year. These ornaments are hung on our "Family Tree," located in our basement family room.

Our five-year-old daughter enjoyed hanging her ornaments on the tree, and we would review who gave her which ornaments or what special event the ornament reminded us of. Last year she hung her ornaments in one clump on the tree, and I had to practice great self-control not to spread them out.

We call our upstairs tree the "Angel Tree," and it is decorated with a variety of angel ornaments I have collected during the past 10 years.

— Connie Faber, Hillsboro, KS

★ The centerpiece of each year's decoration and the first item we hang is a banner that goes over the mantel above the fireplace. It came about that first Christmas in our present home, almost 25 years ago, because I had remnants of white and red faux fur from making a bean bag—red letters on white background with red tassels.

We often place our crèche in a crumbled paper grocery bag or two, made to look like a cave-type stable, with indirect lighting shining on the holy family.

— Marj and Delbert Wiens, Fresno, CA

★ The children know that decorations can go up as soon as we return from Thanksgiving at Grandpop's house. But the rule is—the crèche comes first. Our small artificial tree is safer than a real one because we travel during the Christmas holidays. All the ornaments are gifts, handmade by family members, or souvenirs.

— Donna and John Waldeyer and family, Berwyn, PA

★ In the tropics, we had no spruce or pine trees. Chester gathered branches of native trees and wired them to a wire frame he constructed. Decorations were homemade paper chains, popcorn, and hard candies wrapped in colored paper.

— Sara Jane and Chester Wenger, Lancaster, PA

> ## *"Tree decorating is a friendly, informal way to involve a variety of friends."*

★ My husband Keith teaches elementary school and has collected an assortment of Christmas ornaments given to him by students. He uses these ornaments to decorate a tree in his classroom.

— Gail and Keith Pentz, Casselberry, FL

★ I usually did most of the decorating, but, when it came to the tree, my son Jeff helped me until his late teens. Then he did a bit, but it wasn't his joy. He did enjoy helping to get decorations out each year to see them again. We'd talk about memories. My husband died when he was eight, and so we had Christmas alone most of Jeff's memory years.

— Lil Worley, Homestead, FL

★ Our children loved candlelight suppers from Christmas Eve through New Year's Eve.

— Ellen and Paul Peachey, Harpers Ferry, WV

★ It is fun to go out together to choose just the right tree, but very hard to come to a consensus.

— David and Louisa Mow, Farmington, PA

★ A single friend who has space for a tree made it her tradition to have a bunch of friends over every year for breakfast together, after which we all helped to trim the tree. Other married friends, as well, invited our small group to help their family to decorate their tree. Tree decorating is a friendly, informal way to involve a variety of friends.

— Grace Nolt, Canadensis, PA

★ My husband has a train table that he made. We always had a little tree on top of the table, in the center. The tracks went around the outside. We stacked the wrapped gifts under the table. The sound of that train was very special.
    — Sarah Yoder Scott, Newark, DE

★ Each year we give each child a special ornament—denoting some activity of the child, a remembrance from our family trip of that year, or just an attractive ornament as a keepsake. The ornaments are stored in that child's special box with others he/she made or received through the years. The child places the ornaments on the tree and is responsible for removing them and repacking them. This box will go with the child when the time comes to leave home.
    — Jim and Elaine Gibbel, Lititz, PA

★ We cut stars out of different decorative paper (golden paper, transparent paper) and decorate the windows.
    — Barry, Erika, Karina, and Anya Kreider
    Halle, Germany

★ We use an artificial tree and cover it with lace bows (homemade) and dried weeds (which I gather). Then about two weeks before Christmas, I gather fresh greens (holly, evergreens, etc.) and put them everywhere in the house.
    — Ann Martin, Mount Joy, PA

★ We have a special violin decorated as a door hanging, and we put it on our front door each year. We like to have a potted tree and then plant it outside so we can watch it grow and see the birds build nests in it. For several years in a row we brought the same one indoors. We also have a Moravian star out by our front door each year. I use candles throughout the house, and greens when available.
    — Cathy Boshart, Lebanon, PA

> *"One year our house
> was broken into
> (just before we moved in)
> about two weeks before Christmas,
> and our Christmas ornaments
> were stolen."*

★ We always have a real tree. Sometimes we drop it into the pond to provide a nesting area for fish.
— *Ed and Theo Yoder, Archbold, OH*

★ All the family members help in decorating the house, particularly the young children. We used to prepare the word "STAR" with paper and wooden frame, and put electric balls within it, and then mount it on the top of the house. We also decorate our home with the "greetings" we have received.
— *Thabitha, Daniel R. John Sankararto, Mary S. Rao, Mr. and Mrs. Ron Peters, Gadwal, India*

★ Since our son is a toddler, we chose to put extra lights on the tree (which he enjoys) and only nonbreakable ornaments, so he could play with them. Some of the ornaments are plastic ones which his dad had on the tree when he was little. They are a little "beaten up," but look great and are fun!
— *Sara Zimmerly Ryan, Columbus, OH*

★ We add one new ornament each year that symbolizes something important about the past year.
— *Jim, Lois, Britt, Austin, Reid, and Lane Kaufmann New Paris, IN*

★ On Christmas Eve, we decorate a live tree with lights and dried orange slices. Our grandchildren string a ribbon through pretzels to make a garland. We have greens everywhere.
— *Nancy Riegsecker, Upland, CA*

★ I have gradually collected a variety of angels which decorate the tree and other areas of the house. Each year I like to add one or two new ones.
—*Hildegarde Baerg, Abbotsford, British Columbia*

★ We use a manger scene made from a hollow log from our woods.
—*Arnold and Mary K. Regier, West Liberty, OH*

★ One year our house was broken into (just before we moved in) about two weeks before Christmas, and our Christmas ornaments were stolen. Our church small group pitched in and gave us ornaments, which are doubly meaningful now because of that memory.
—*Rod and Martha Yoder Maust, Indianapolis, IN*

★ I have three fireplace mantels which I decorate in different themes. The living room mantel is in classic wine and burgundy ribbons, berries, pinecones, beads, and a string of tiny white lights.

This year I did the dining room mantel with a gold theme. I spray painted old dried fruit, acorns, pinecones, and old tree ornaments which had become discolored and moldy. I could not find gold wooden beads, so I took a string of red wooden beads and placed it into a plastic bag, together with all the other items I sprayed gold. It turned out to be wonderful. The beads and a gold ribbon, rippling across the boughs, added a great finish.

The family room fireplace I decorated in the traditional green boughs, with tiny colored or white lights and the favorite wooden tree ornaments the children grew up with, as well as the red wooden beads, pine cones, and ribbons trailing across. I generally scrounge the neighborhood or parks for berries and add them to all my bough decorations.

We always plant amaryllis and paper whites every November so we have fresh colorful flowers over Christmas.

The poinsettias are also an annual addition. My Christmas cactus plants generally cooperate and bloom close to Christmas, as do my many African violets and hibiscus trees.

I ask friends, relatives, and neighbors to collect bits and pieces of old, burned down candles which I melt down, clean, and prepare for new candles. I decorate the entire house with them. This year I made two dozen. And as the need arises, I take one and wrap it for a gift to give to someone.
— *Norma J. Pauls, Oakville, Ontario*

★ We have made a commitment to use only a living ball-root tree—and sometimes have had none at all, when a live tree wasn't possible—in which case our decorations were simply hung gaily throughout the room.

Whenever possible, we decorate last year's tree, which is now planted outside, sometimes including popcorn strings and bread crumbs for the animals and birds to nibble.

We have also brought a fallen branch of a deciduous tree inside and decorated it, and have found that to be quite beautiful. Using only white lights and old-fashioned silver beads with our regular decorations, the tree was enchanting. "It looks like a tree from an old-fashioned mansion," said my youngest!

Others we know decorate huge tumbleweed skeletons or wrap vines and moss tightly into a large cone shape and deco-

rate that. We understand that here on the prairie where we live, the pioneers never cut living trees at Christmas, because trees were so scarce, and instead used fallen branches or tumbleweeds. We enjoy continuing that practice.

We also have a pinecone collection we get out at Christmas and use as a centerpiece. We have cones gathered from all over the U.S. on our travels: the Sierras, the high plateaus of New Mexico, etc. All sizes and shapes—and we keep gathering as we go!
— *Kirsten Zerger, McPherson, KS*

★ We place our gifts around a "manger" which reminds us of God's best gift to us. Instead of a tree, we empty our antique dough tray and use it for a manger. Sometimes we use a black baby Jesus; sometimes a white one. Sometimes I use greens around the baby instead of straw. We use a lot of fresh greens—outdoors on window ledges and indoors on the mantel, in baskets and in centerpieces with candles.
— *Erma Wenger, Lancaster, PA*

★ Our crèche is a focal point of the dining room. Most of the pieces have been collected over the years from the local Self-Help shop, which markets crafts made all over the world. The stable is from Laos; Mary, Joseph, and Jesus are from Mexico; the star is an ornament from India. Each year we add an animal to pack into the stable. There's a wooden goat from Haiti, a mother and baby llama from Peru, a soapstone sheep from Kenya, a handsewn muslin dove from an aunt, a bird from Mexico, a deer from Chile (from a UNICEF shop), and an owl perched on the roof. Somehow it seems very fitting to have many cultures represented at the manger.
— *Matthew, Barbara, Stephen, and Naomi Woolsey Batavia, NY*

> *"It was a nice discovery to find*
> *that the quality of our tree*
> *is not as important*
> *as the quality*
> *of our relationships."*

★ Decorations for our Christmas tree have varied: one year, small wreaths made of lace and ribbon on a plastic ring were handcrafted; another year little angels made of a variety of pastas were the only decorations; sometimes a variety of handmade items plus some wooden figures, brass items, and small colorful balls were used; one year German pincher-type candleholders with wax candles were used. (These were lovely when lit, but we felt unsafe and did that only one year!)

We always place a small handmade ceramic tree with multicolored umbrella tips to represent lights on a table or bookcase each Christmas season.

—*Richard and Betty Pellman, Millersville, PA*

★ Our family harvested a pine tree from our farm each year. Since the trees had not been trimmed, imperfect branches left gaping spaces between yearly levels of growth. Garlands, tinsel, and ornaments did help fill in the empty spaces, and a bird nest tucked in the branches added interest. But the trees were not exactly works of art.

One year our daughter in college decided that we needed a thick, symmetrical tree. She and I followed directions to a tree farm. It was dusk when we reached the place. Although they were already closed, they graciously invited me in to visit with Granny by the fireplace while they took our daughter out to cut a tree. It was gorgeous! For one holiday season we celebrated like other people. And we repeated this for several years following.

Then this year she and her brother didn't get home until shortly before Christmas. We found another tree on our farm that resembled our previous trees. When we brought it in, no one complained about the skimpy branches. We were too busy visiting while we all joined in, stringing cranberries to help to fill the empty spots. We thought it looked quite rustic.

It was a nice discovery to find that the quality of our tree is not as important as the quality of our relationships.

—*John and Trula Zimmerly, Jackson, OH*

★ In the last 17 years, we have had many international students from many different countries spend two weeks with us over the Christmas holiday. A lot of our decorations are gifts from these young people.

Our tree is not beautifully decorated with red bows and crystal angels—it is a hodgepodge of love. A crocheted bell from friend Ruth, a ceramic bell with granddaughter Emily's baby picture glued to it (she's 13 now—but still looks to see if I include it each year), two bamboo angels from Shin-li from Taiwan, a stuffed cardinal from Zelda, three-headed ornaments made by my 83-year-old mother.

As I decorate the tree with these and many more, I breathe a prayer for each giver and feel very loved as the recipient of such wonderful memories!

—*Annabelle and Dan Unternahrer, Shipshewana, IN*

★ I've gradually added decorations over the years, some of which I've made, such as things from old Christmas cards. This includes small boxes, a round ball, and a star with 20 points. We also have pictures glued onto old canning lids which we hang on a white birch branch cut fresh each year and placed in an old crock. (Some of these things I've also made and given as gifts.)

On our fireplace mantel we place a wooden, handcrafted sleigh and reindeer set which a dear friend gave me some 30 years ago. I wrap tiny little boxes and pile them in the sleigh.

— Ernestine and Keith Lehman and family, Lititz, PA

★ In our area, there are a number of sizable weeds. Some people decorate tumbleweed. We've found another weed, a tall one with a strong stem and wispy "branches." We "prune" it and decorate it with mini lights and lightweight ornaments.

— Ben and Eunice Stoner, Farmington, NM

★ Instead of a Christmas tree, we place the focus on nativity scenes. We don't set up a tree at all, but arrange our five nativity sets around our main living area and accent them with strategically placed candles. We place our gifts in front of the main olive wood nativity. The concrete image reminds us that what we have has been given to us by God, and that our gifts, in turn, are for the good of God.

— Suzanne Marie Hitt, Fairfield, OH

★ One year was a lean year, and we had a large branch we decorated. It did not deter from the excitement. We have photos of the children on Christmas morning in their pajamas, exclaiming over their gifts and the "tree."

— Merv and Gladys Rutt, Blue Ball, PA

★ Our six-year-old son enjoys looking at photo ornaments he's made with preschool photos from earlier years.

— Carol and Jim Spicher, Mountville, PA

★ Our whole family joins with our church tree-cutting outing in the first week of December. We drive into the hills (an event in itself). Each family cuts its own tree. We always get an extra permit and bring a tree for Oma and Opa. For lunch we light a huge bonfire and roast wieners on sticks. We begin the "meal" with a praise song and a prayer. (The only time I miss the event is when I babysit a grandchild.)
—*Jake and Herta Janzen, Coledale, Alberta*

★ Two years in a row, a single friend who is gifted artistically helped our children to make ornaments from bread dough. These are painted and varnished, and hold special memories of those years.
—*Jewel Showalter, Landisville, PA*

★ As the children were given or made ornaments over the years, we began packing the ornaments accordingly. So we have a box for each child, separate from the family ornaments. When they leave home, their boxes are all ready for them to take with them to decorate their own first trees.
—*Jane Hoober Peifer, Harrisonburg, VA*

★   My husband, being an electrician, built a large star, lit with blue Christmas bulbs. This was a project father and sons did together. The star goes up every year, telling the world that Jesus is born.
—Miriam E. Umble, Parkesburg, PA

★   Decorating begins Thanksgiving weekend. Our children are still too young to help, but I enjoy making things. This year I made a nativity scene that small children can play with.
—Joe and Laura Bare, New Braunfels, TX

★   Branches of pine across our mantel, colored lights, and memoirs from throughout the years have long been our substitute for a Christmas tree. Add to that lots of candles throughout the house with sprigs of holly and pine, and it's festive and pretty. (I feel badly about all the trees waiting for the waste management truck the day after Christmas!)
—Michael, Lena, Lowell, and Miriam Brown
Grantham, PA

★   One of my best-ever decorations was the year I used a tinsel garland to string up a star in my front window on the grating. Then I strung small lights along the path.
—E. Elaine Kauffman, Campinas, Brazil

★ Since my husband died three years ago, my young son and daughter have been extremely helpful in trimming the tree with lights and ornaments. The three wise men, made over 30 years ago, have a special place in our in-house decorating, as does a lovely nativity set.

—Louise Auernheimer, Reedley, CA

★ Jim's mother made us decorations out of milkweed pods in which she put angel hair and a tiny angel or baby Jesus figure.

—Helen and James Reusser, Kitchener, Ontario

★ Dean and I were married on December 2 and had Christmas trees at our wedding.

Since then, we've kept the tradition of setting up our family Christmas tree over our anniversary. Instead of roses, he buys me several red poinsettias to kick off the decorating.

—Jan Steffy Mast, Lancaster, PA

★ We have a tradition of setting up a small crèche made 40 years ago by father and son.

—Eloise Sommers, Lakewood, CO

★ Even though our children are older and mostly away from home, they enjoy having their childhood ornaments on display. I have an old high-top desk which I empty. Then I open the glass door and put many of these "old" things on display there, with lights.

—Jon and Esther Bucher, Marinville, Alberta

★ We all work together, remaking homemade ornaments and decorations. Our five-year-old took it upon herself to wind red yarn around all the railings for our cathedral ceiling and stairs. Thanks to her abundant use of yarn and paper, we have a well adorned house!

We also all help to set up the manager scene in our

quaint stable-barn together. All help to rearrange the characters many times a day. We even discovered that, with a Lego electric unit, we could have a flashing star!

We also set aside one Sunday afternoon during Advent to make candles together. We dip candles and make molded candle creations. Somehow those candles have so much more character and feeling to them than the perfect tapers we buy from the store!

—*Helen Stoltzfus Bowman, Millersburg, IN*

---

*"The night
we decorate the tree,
we have gingerbread waffles,
cream sauce,
and fruit salad."*

★   We decorate inside our finch's cage with a miniature Christmas tree, tiny glass balls, and colorful plastic holly. During the holidays we line the cage with used giftwrap, salvaged from the previous Christmas. For a Christmas treat, our bird gets sprays of millet to eat. Our cat receives fresh fish for his Christmas Eve supper. At bedtime we pray for "every living thing" in our home (including plants and pets) to be blessed by God.

Every year we put homemade pillar candles on the windowsills and on top of our bookcases, surrounded by beds of greenery. We light the candles, along with Great-Great Grandpa's oil lamp, only on Christmas Eve. We do not light the set of nativity candle figures Mom made 20 years ago, but we display it annually on an African scarf sent by a missionary friend many Christmases ago.

—*Dawn Pichette, Harbor City, CA*

> *"For a Christmas treat,*
> *our bird gets sprays of millet*
> *to eat.*
> *Our cat receives*
> *fresh fish*
> *for his Christmas Eve supper."*

★ I like to collect angels to display. They remind me of many aspects of the Christmas story—the miracle of Jesus' birth, and the joy brought to all people.

We like to display all the colorful cards we receive by hanging them on a long ribbon. After the holidays, we put the cards in a basket on the kitchen table and choose a card each night at supper. We remember the family or individual who sent the card in prayer around the supper table.
— *Ned and Debbi Wyse, Camden, MI*

★ The night we decorate the tree, we have gingerbread waffles, cream sauce, and fruit salad.
— *Julie Vlasits, Keezletown, VA*

★ When the children were young, we made a piñata every year with papier-mâché. All the younger generation (cousins) got involved in the activity, trying to break it while blindfolded. The preparation was a long process, so it created a lot of anticipation.

I made a huge star—about eight feet tall—of metal and trimmed full of lights which we mount on top of our house (which is on a hill overlooking our town).

I use the beautiful Christmas cards which we've gathered for years to make wonderful placemats which we use every year—and have given as gifts. To make them, cut tagboard (or something similar) to placemat size, choose and place cards artistically, and lightly glue them in place. In the early years I used contact paper to cover them, which was a mess. More recently I laminate them with plastic. This works much better. Most of ours have Christmas greetings, blessings, prayers, and quotes. We enjoy these very much, and others often remark on their beauty and usefulness.

—Jeanette Ediger Flaming, Dallas, OR

★   We started making our own Christmas decorations out of necessity—our budget didn't allow for buying such "nonessentials." We're still making them, but out of choice now. Decorations made years ago and still used today are reminders of Christmases past.

During one of our first years of marriage, I made three choirgirls by folding the pages of *Reader's Digest* magazines, spraying them red and gold, and placing a head made with a styrofoam ball on top of each. I cut construction paper for their robe arms, and for a song book titled "The First Noel."

Today, five choirgirls are part of our Christmas decorations (some are the original ones—beginning to look their age, I might add).

Candles are part of most of our Christmas decorations, and we make most of them. We use wax from old candles—our own, some given by friends, or others found at the local thrift store.

The smell of melting wax is part of our Christmas. In addition to using molds and hand dipping, we make snowball and chimney candles. An old, small, hollow rubber ball, cut in half, is a great mold for snowball candles.

The paper juice cartons used in school are perfect as disposable molds for the red chimney candles. The box can simply be torn away when the candle hardens. We etch "bricks" on all four sides of the candle with an ice pick. Whipped white wax covers the top and drips down over the side, making these little chimneys look snow-covered.

—Sarah and Herb Myers, Mount Joy, PA

★ One year when our five children were small and we had access to clay and a kiln, we made a circle scene, each person creating several figures. That scene is a treasured family possession, with its cow with a crumpled horn, knobby donkey, sheep, shepherds, kings, camels, and a sweet-faced Mary, Joseph, and baby Jesus.

We bring it out each year shortly after the Advent wreath. Those are our only decorations until about a week before Christmas when we put up a small live tree and a pine spray I make for the doors.

—Hazel L. Miller, Hudson, IL

★ We constructed a simple wooden decoration of the manger and cross that we hang and then spotlight on the front of our house.

—Ann and Byron Weber Becker, Kitchener, Ontario

★ We collect antique decorations. On the walls, for example, we have a collection of 1876 to 1886 *Harper's Weekly*, framed with Christmas illustrations from artists like Thomas Nast.

—Dale and Rosie Horst, Newton, KS

★ Often our family got a permit from the nearby forest reserve to cut a Christmas tree. Other times we selected one as a family from a tree lot. The tree is decorated by as many members of the family as can be home for the occasion. Our ornaments reflect part of our family history.

—Justina M. Heese, Steinbach, Manitoba

★ We five women (four daughters and Mom) put up all the decorations the Friday and Saturday after Thanksgiving, when Dad goes hunting.
— *Abbie Berkshire, Harrisonburg, VA*

★ We like to use lights around our windows and several places in our house. And we like to leave them up until March, when the days (and daylight) have gotten longer.
— *Stan, Carol, Sarah, and Ben Miller Histand*
Soldotna, AK

★ As a variation from the traditional Christmas tree, we often buy eight or 10 poinsettias and arrange them as a tree.
— *Alice and Willard Roth, Elkhart, IN*

2.

Food Ideas
and Traditions

★ One of our favorite food traditions as a family is our Christmas Eve fondue dinner. For the first course we serve cheese fondue, into which we dip French bread chunks, black olives, raw broccoli, celery, cauliflower, and smoked sausage. Our second course is a chocolate fondue with chunks of apples, bananas, oranges, pineapple, and grapes.

We use our best china and goblets and eat by candlelight, even though fondue itself is an informal kind of meal and a lot of fun.

—*Jim, Lois, Britt, Austin, Reid, and Lane Kaufmann*
New Paris, IN

★ At Christmas-time we eat watermelon in the shade of our mulberry tree! Our nine-year-old twins were drawing Christmas pictures, and Hannah pictured the family sitting in the shade of the tree, eating watermelon. Christmas falls in summer here, at the beginning of watermelon season.
— *Becky Wigginton, Chaco, Argentina*

★ Our two children, ages two and five, love to help me bake. The week before we put up our Christmas tree, the kids help me bake our first batch of Christmas cookies, usually sugar cookies. The kids like to put lots of colored sugar and sprinkles on them.

Then on the night we decorate our tree, we get out those sugar cookies and put them on our Christmas tray to nibble on while we decorate. The kids are tempted to pull out all the decorations at once, but the cookie tray distracts them while Daddy unravels the lights.

Usually we have eggnog with our cookies, as well. It's a festive way to make decorating the tree less frustrating. It also motivates me to start cookie-baking earlier than I used to.
— *Doug and Dawn Nyce, Lancaster, PA*

★ A tradition we started about 10 years ago was NOT to have a large Christmas dinner. Our family gathers together for a Christmas Eve soup supper before church. On

Christmas Day, we snack on the leftovers from Christmas Eve, brunch food, and all the other "goodies" everyone seems to have around during this season. It has been a wonderful thing, at least for our family, to free ourselves from all the cooking and to spend the day more restfully.

> — *Clark, Cindy, Lara, and Hilary Breeze*
> *Champaign, IL*

★ When it snows for the first time each winter, we have apple dumplings and vanilla sauce in the evening.

> — *Barry, Erika, Karina, and Anya Kreider*
> *Halle, Germany*

★ We sometimes make our own cookie designs. We made dinosaur cookie shapes one year—a hit with both young and old.

> — *Beth Weaver Bonnar, Nelson, British Columbia*

★ Our daughter hosted our Christmas Eve meal this year. She started several months ahead of time, finding different books and magazines with recipes for the type of food she wanted to serve buffet style. She hunted recipes for finger foods, dips, and sauces, both hot and cold. She tried these new recipes and everyone liked the variation.

> — *Joyce Eigsti Hofer, Denver, CO*

★ We put roasted pig, "patupat" (a rice cake cooked in a coconut leaf-wrapper), all kinds of rice cakes, and fruits out on a table so that all passersby can help themselves. We do this only once a year.

> — *Luis A. Lumibao, San Jose City, Philippines*

★ Each family member brings his/her favorite food, gift wrapped and identified by name to our get-together. The youngest picks a gift, other than his/her own, and opens it. The person who brought that gift opens the next one, and so on. All the food gifts must be the kind that can be prepared

in 10 minutes or less, so the meal being given can be eaten without a long delay!
— *J. Allen and Erma Brubaker, Lancaster, PA*

★ Our four-year-old daughter insisted on a birthday cake for baby Jesus, complete with singing "Happy Birthday." I think that activity helps to keep young children focused on the meaning of Christmas.
— *Karl and Marcia Brubaker, Goessel, KS*

★ In the Lehman family, it has become a tradition to have a dinner with spiced shrimp. Mom Lehman buys the shrimp (25 lb. for 45 people) and my husband, Galen, prepares it. The grandchildren are happy to attend a family gathering with a special food like shrimp. Even though the expense is high, Mom feels it provides an incentive for the children and grandchildren to plan their schedules so they can come. Ham is also served, along with green beans, baked corn, potato salad, and cookies.
— *Gloria Lehman, Singers Glen, VA*

★ We buy pecan products from Koinonia Partners in Americus, Georgia, to give as gifts. They are tasty and much appreciated as gifts, and we get the satisfaction of knowing we're helping a good cause.
— *Rod and Martha Yoder Maust, Indianapolis, IN*

★ We always make bread for our eight to 10 closest neighbors. On our more energetic years, we also gave each a pint of pear butter, made from the pear tree in our backyard, which these same neighbors eat pears from earlier in the year. The children love to help us to deliver the gifts.

One of our favorite traditions, before we had children, was to have a chocolate fondue party with friends in the middle of our living room floor. While we dipped bits of fruit into the melted chocolate, we took turns reading *The Best Christmas Pageant Ever* to each other. It was a time to enjoy

good company, good food and laughs, and to hear the Christmas story, again, for the first time!
— *John and Sandra Drescher-Lehman, Richmond, VA*

★ Though sharing food with our neighbors is common practice here, during Christmas season we prepare simple new recipes from different cultures (Indonesia is an archipelago with over 200 different cultures). We share them with our close friends and neighbors. With sensitivity, we also share our reflections, along with Christmas greetings.
— *Charles and Lisa Christano, Kudus, Indonesia*

★ We like to make fudge to give as gifts.
— *Kym Sutter, Manson, IA*

★ My mom always serves cranberries and sauerkraut with turkey. And we have a baked Alaska for Christmas dessert.
— *The Baker-Smiths, Waitsburg, WA*

★ We bake cookies and sometimes make miniature loaves of nut bread to give to friends and co-workers. Our favorite cookie recipe is Russian Tea Cakes.
— *Keith and Gail Pentz, Casselberry, FL*

Russian Tea Cakes

1 cup soft butter   2¼ cups flour
½ cup confectioner's sugar ¼ tsp. salt
1 tsp. vanilla   ¾ cup finely chopped nuts

1. Cream butter, sugar, and vanilla
2. Blend in flour and salt. Stir in nuts.
3. Chill dough.
4. Roll into 1" balls. Bake 10-12 minutes at 400°.
5. Roll the cookies in confectioner's sugar as soon as they come out of the oven. Roll them in confectioner's sugar again when they are cool.

★ For our main celebration meal as a family we feast on exotic, spicy Ethiopian Injera and Wat. We lived in Ethiopia while our children were growing up.
— *Chester and Sara Jane Wenger, Lancaster, PA*

Injera
Makes 20 12" Injera

3 cups flour
½ cup whole wheat flour
½ cup cornmeal or
   masa harina

1 Tbsp. active dry yeast
3½ cups warm water

1. Mix all ingredients together. Let set in large bowl, covered, an hour or longer, until batter rises and becomes stretchy. (It can sit as long as 3-6 hours.)
2. When ready, stir batter if liquid has settled on bottom. Then whip in blender, 2 cups batter at a time, thinning it with ½-¾ cup water. Batter will be quite thin.
3. Cook in nonstick frypan without oil over medium or medium-high heat. Use ½ cup batter per Injera for 12" pan or ⅓ cup batter per Injera for 10" pan.

Pour batter into heated pan and quickly swirl pan to spread batter as thin as possible. Batter should be no thicker than ⅛". Do not turn.

Injera does not easily stick or burn. It is cooked through when bubbles appear all over top.
4. Lay each Injera on a clean towel for a minute or two, then stack in covered dish to keep warm. Finished Injera will be thicker than a crepe, but thinner than a pancake.
5. To serve, overlap a few Injera on large platter and place stews on top. Or lay one Injera on each dinner plate and ladle stew servings on top. Give each person three or more Injera, rolled or folded in quarters, to use for scooping up the stews.

Chicken Wat
Makes 4 servings

2½-3 lbs. chicken pieces
2 Tbsp. lemon juice
1 tsp. salt
2 Tbsp. margarine
2 cups onions, chopped
1 Tbsp. garlic, minced
1 tsp. ginger root, grated
¼ tsp. fenugreek, crushed

¼ tsp. ground cardamom
⅛ tsp. ground nutmeg
¼ cup Berbere
2 Tbsp. paprika
½ cup water
1 hard-cooked egg
   for each person

1. Remove skin from chicken pieces. Sprinkle with lemon juice and salt. Let stand while preparing other ingredients.
2. Melt margarine in large saucepan. Add onions, garlic, and ginger root, and cook until softened but not browned.
3. Stir in next 3 ingredients. Then add next 2 ingredients and stir over low heat 2-3 minutes.
4. Pour in water. Bring to a boil over high heat, stirring continuously.
5. Add chicken to sauce, turning pieces until all are coated. Reduce heat to medium low, cover, and simmer until chicken is tender, about 45 minutes, turning once or twice to coat chicken evenly. If it becomes too dry, add a little water. Sauce should be consistency of heavy cream.
6. Cut shallow slits in each hard-cooked egg to allow color and flavor of sauce to permeate. Add eggs to sauce and simmer 10 minutes. Stew can be made a day ahead of time and refrigerated. Add eggs when reheating.

★ Cookie baking was and is always a part of our holiday preparation. One year, because I had been hospitalized prior to Christmas, the children, with my guidance, made the cookies *after* Christmas while they were on vacation. It actually turned out to be a highlight!

The past several years our family has requested pig stomach stuffed with a potato sausage filling, instead of turkey, so that has become our tradition.

— Betty and Richard Pellman, Millersville, PA

★ I usually bake eight to 10 different kinds of cookies in the weeks after Thanksgiving and freeze them. We then make up gift plates of cookies for teachers, Sunday school teachers, neighbors, and friends and deliver them. Of course, we eat some every day, and take platters of cookies to family gatherings.

Some I bake are Lebkuchen, crescent or wedding cakes, sand tarts, Christmas shortbread, cream cheese, pecan tassies, Italian stars, sugar balls, peppernuts, and springerle. (I like using the springerle molds I got in Germany and Switzerland, and the cookies are fun to make and pretty, even though our family doesn't care for the taste very much.)

Sand tarts are always a part of Christmas. I do the mixing, rolling, and most of the cutting. Jim and the children decorate. What a mix of colors when the children were young! This year Ethan, 15, decorated and supervised the oven, too—they were beautiful cookies!

— Elaine and Jim Gibbel, Lititz, PA

★ Over the years we gradually adopted a menu for Christmas dinner that never changes. It consists of hot rolls, sliced ham, sweet potatoes, cranberry salad, a vegetable, oyster dressing, and Christmas cookies with ice cream or sherbet.

The specialty is the Oyster Dressing.

— John and Trula Zimmerly, Jackson, OH

Oyster Dressing

1½ sticks (12 Tbsp.)   1 pint oysters with liquid
   butter or margarine   3-4 cups milk
¾ lb. saltine crackers   salt to taste

1. Melt 6 Tbsp. butter in baking dish. Set aside.
2. Crush crackers.
3. Melt remaining 6 Tbsp. butter and mix with crushed crackers, oysters and liquid, milk, and salt to taste.
4. Pour over melted butter in baking dish.
5. Bake at 350° for 1 hour or until golden brown.

★   I have found Lemon Loaf to be a wonderful gift bread. I have yet to meet someone who doesn't like it.
— *Matthew, Barbara, Stephen, and Naomi Woolsey*
Batavia, NY

Lemon Loaf
Makes 2 loaves

2 cups sugar   2½ cups white flour
3 eggs   2 tsp. baking powder
1 cup margarine, melted   1 cup milk
½ cup potato flour*   rind of 1 lemon, grated

1. Beat sugar and eggs together until thick.
2. Add the rest of the ingredients and mix them until they are blended.
3. Grease and flour only the bottoms of two loaf pans. Pour half the batter into each pan.
4. Bake at 350° 50-60 minutes.
5. Remove from pans. While still warm, glaze with a thick paste of **juice from 1 lemon** and **confectioner's sugar.**

* Potato flour is similar to cornstarch and gives this cake a smooth texture. If it is not available, substitute cornstarch or rice flour, or increase white flour to 3 cups.

★ For three or four generations, our family has gotten together and made chocolate-covered candies. This year we made 150 lbs. of it.
— *Ann Martin, Mount Joy, PA*

★ I usually make a variety of Christmas cookies, both to give away and to serve to visitors. We have a favorite activity that can be used with any rolled-out dough. Place tin foil on cookie sheet. Lay cut-out sugar cookies on the foil. Cut small holes in each cookie with a bottle top, thimble, orange corer, or whatever you have on hand. Fill the holes with mounds of crushed hard candy. Use any colorful hard candy that is clear, not cloudy. Bake the cookies as usual. Slip foil off the cookie sheet so you can re-use the sheet while the cookies cool. Wait until the candy centers are set before peeling cookies off foil. These make lovely "stained glass window" cookies for eating or decorating a tree.
— *Jeanne Shirk Sahawneh, Irbid, Jordan*

★ My granddaughter asked me this year, "Grandma, why don't you make those Holly Wreaths you used to make?"
So next year we will have Holly Wreaths for Christmas.
— *Marjora Miller, Archbold, OH*

★ We always have Christmas breakfast together as a family, even though none of us children lives at home anymore. The meal is cheese ball, crackers, fruit, egg custard, and juice.
— *Dawn J. Ranck, Strasburg, PA*

★ Christmas meal is not complete without sweet potato soufflé.
— *Mrs. Miriam Shoup, Orrville, OH*

★ Baklava (greek pastry) has become a tradition at Christmas for our family.
— *Heidi Eash, Bristol, IN*

Holly Wreaths

½ cup butter or margarine
3 cups miniature
   marshmallows
½ tsp. vanilla

1½ tsp. green food coloring
3½ cups cornflakes
red hots

1. Melt butter and marshmallows together over low heat.
2. Add vanilla and food coloring.
3. Fold in cornflakes.
4. Shape mixture into wreaths on greased pans or waxed paper.
5. Decorate with red hots.

— Marjora Miller, Archbold, OH

Variation:

Press warm cornflake mixture into 6-cup ring mold or shape into a ring on a serving plate. Use it as a centerpiece with a candle in the middle. Remove from the mold and slice to serve.

—Leona and Paul Bender, Belleville, PA

★ For our family Christmas dinner we always have cold, sliced, baked ham, with horseradish available for those who want to clear their sinuses. Every Christmas, someone in the family makes a large kettle of pluma-mooss, a porridge with raisins, plums, and cinnamon sticks. We serve it along with the ham and (usually) hash brown potatoes.

—Wilmer A. and Esther M. Harms
North Newton, KS

Pluma-Mooss

2 cups raisins
1½ cups dried prunes
8 cups water
cream
½ cup flour
½ cup sugar

½ tsp. salt
2 Tbsp. vinegar
2 cups half-and-half or

2 sticks cinnamon
2 whole star anise

1. In a large saucepan or kettle combine fruit and water and bring to a boil. Simmer until almost tender.
2. Make a paste with the flour, sugar, salt, vinegar, and cream. Add paste to fruit slowly, stirring constantly until mixture comes to a boil.
3. Add cinnamon and anise and continue boiling about 5 minutes. Remove from heat and cool. May be served warm or cold.

Hint: Mooss may be made thinner by adding a little extra water when cooking the fruit.

★ My mother always made a variety of candies—no cookies. So caramel corn is a yearly tradition, and we have used it as a Christmas gift. We make traditional soft caramels; we melt chocolate and mix the cereal, Kix, with it or pieces of walnuts or hickory nuts, dripping them in small clusters onto waxed paper.

We usually eat breakfast on Christmas Day during the late morning and have our big meal of the day between two and three in the afternoon. Between the two meals, I sometimes serve a sherbet-cream punch and some munchies.

— *Ernestine and Keith Lehman and family, Lititz, PA*

Sherbet-Cream Punch
Serves 20

10½ cups pineapple juice*   **1¼ cups vanilla ice cream**
1½ pints orange sherbet   **4½ cups chilled ginger ale**

Mix first 3 ingredients together gently. When sherbet and ice cream are softened, add ginger ale and serve.

* 1 quart pineapple juice=5¾ cups.

★ Every year we have a "Cookie Day." All our daughters and daughters-in-law come home. Each brings supplies, and some have dough all prepared. We bake the whole day and divide the cookies among our seven families. Last year we baked about 2,000 cookies. They were beautiful, all lined up on our big dining room table. My husband usually helps; he takes them off the pans and arranges them to cool.

— *Sarah Yoder Scott, Newark, DE*

★ We take oranges around to our neighborhood households and give a navel orange for each person living in each house. This provides a link with neighbors, however brief, but does connect us when the weather is cold and we tend to stay in our houses. A few are ready for us with a plate of cookies. We were surprised when this first happened, as we were not giving to receive, but it seemed like they felt better if they could also give something to us.

— *Barbara Longenecker, New Holland, PA*

★ We send food gifts to our friends and neighbors, whether they celebrate Christmas or not.
> — *Thabitha, Daniel, and R. John Sankararto, Mary S. Rao, Mr. and Mrs. Ron Peters, Gadwal, India*

★ A new "tradition" has started for us this year. Recently we have discovered wild plums. Though they are rather tart, we canned several quarts. The grandchildren like them like this, but the skins are still pretty tart for most of us. We decided to try some in fruitcake. Everyone loves it!

Here's the recipe for our "Wild Plum Fruitcake."
> — *John and Betty Wittrig, Winfield, IA*

Wild Plum Fruitcake

1½ cups whole wheat
  pastry flour
1 tsp. ground cinnamon
½ tsp. baking powder
¼ tsp. ground nutmeg
1 cup canned wild plums,
  pitted and diced
½ cup raisins
8 oz. diced, pitted dates
½ orange peel,
  chopped fine

3 oz. walnuts, chopped
3 oz. pecans chopped
3 eggs
½ cup brown sugar
  or honey
½ cup orange juice
⅓ cup butter, melted
2 Tbsp. molasses
2 Tbsp. maple syrup

1. Combine flour and all other dry ingredients.
2. Add fruits, peels, and nuts, and mix well.
3. Beat eggs. Stir in sugar, juice, butter, and syrups and combine with rest of ingredients.
4. Pour into greased 8" x 4" loaf pan. Bake at 275° for 1½ hours.
5. Eat when cool, or wrap in fruit-juice-moistened cheese-cloth in refrigerator for 2 to 6 weeks.

★ We bake fruitcakes in foil pans. Then we can easily mail them to relatives and friends. The cakes can be made as early as November or October, and they won't spoil or get stale by the holidays.

> — *David and Louisa Mow, Farmington, PA*

★ The Monday after Thanksgiving, when the children have the day off from school, we enjoy baking sand tarts at Grandma's house. In addition to the sand tarts, I keep four other cookie recipes and two shortbread recipes that we make only at Christmas-time. We make several batches of each and place them promptly into the freezer so they don't disappear before Christmas!

During Christmas week, we prepare plates of cookies for extended family, neighbors, and co-workers. Everyone anticipates their "favorite" kind! (I hear about it if they are late arriving!)

> — *Stephanie, Dale, Ashley, and Zachary Kaufman Strasburg, PA*

★ We buy and deliver a food basket for a needy family in our county.

> — *Susan and Michael Davis, Brentwood, TN*

★ Last Christmas our daughter Linda wrote in preparation for her coming home for the holiday, "Let's have plum pudding." For more years than not, our Christmas dinners were topped with a flaming, steamed English plum pudding, decorated with holly berries from our backyard. We were all too full, of course, to eat more than a taste, until the next day.
— *Marj and Delbert Wiens, Fresno, CA*

★ Our family Christmas meal is traditionally turkey, served with a cranberry salad. Three kinds of cookies are a must— sugar cookies with icing (cut in the form of trees, stars, angels, etc.), Russian tea cakes, and date balls.

My mother always baked a fruitcake, made with raisins, currants, nuts, apples, and citron. She brought it to the table only once—after that it was reserved as small treats for the children.
— *Esther and Linden Wenger, Harrisonburg, VA*

★ We always have French onion soup before we open our gifts. And we serve date pudding and graham cracker fluff only at Christmas.
— *Theo and Ed Yoder, Archbold, OH*

★ Christmas pudding is a tradition at our house. I usually make either a plum or carrot pudding early in December. I fill empty 14-ounce vegetable tins with the batter, then steam six of them at a time in my large steamer. (A large kettle may also be used as a steamer.)

These individual puddings, along with jars of lemon or butterscotch sauce, make nice gifts for neighbors and colleagues at work.
— *Miriam and Howard Cressman*
Cambridge, Ontario

★ I bake several kinds of Christmas cookies and breads, especially Brown Bread and Cinnamon-Sugar Loaf.
— *Faye Nyce, Grantham, PA*

Brown Bread
3 1-lb. loaves

1½ cups seedless raisins	1 egg
1½ cups water	2 tsp. melted shortening
2 tsp. baking soda	2¾ cups flour
1 cup sugar	pinch of salt

1. Mix raisins and water together in a saucepan. Bring to a boil. Add baking soda while fruit is still hot.
2. Stir in remaining ingredients and blend well.
3. Grease 3 1-lb. cans; then fill each ⅔ full.
4. Bake at 350° for 1 hour.
5. Lay cans on sides to cool.

★ On Christmas Eve, we bake Christmas bread. We form it into a wreath. The wreath becomes a centerpiece when we place our German candleholder with angels on the inside. When the candles burn, the angels fly in a circle, ringing two bells. We eat the bread/centerpiece after church on Christmas Eve.

We make a number of food gifts throughout the year. We have the good fortune of living in an area with abundant fresh berries in the summer, so we try to put up a number of different kinds of jam. Our favorites are strawberry (from our friends' fields), raspberry (from Grandma's yard), and black-berry (from just about anywhere!). We preserve them in small jars. These make great gifts, either by themselves or in gift baskets.

Another food tradition in our house is to make Christmas Granola. We use a basic granola recipe and always add at least three kinds of dried fruit. The fruits vary according to what we've dried that year, but we always put in a generous amount of dried strawberries, giving the granola a beautiful touch of red. This has been a well-received gift for a number of years.

— *Gwen Gustafson-Zook, Portland, OR*

★ We always look forward to oysters and fresh mushrooms. We either fry the oysters or make them into an oyster stew to be served sometime over the holidays. We have friends from "mushroom country" in Chester County, PA, who give us a box of fresh mushrooms each year.

— *Jane Hoober Peifer, Harrisonburg, VA*

★ We have a Christmas Eve tradition of eating oyster stew with accompanying snacks, such as a relish plate, bean dip, cheese log and crackers, and sparkling grape juice.

Without doubt, we have the *best* peppernut recipe! It's an old Showalter family favorite. Sometimes we make as many as three or four batches throughout the season. It's a project that has involved family members since they were toddlers—and we've passed the recipe on to many friends who have shared Christmas with us. Jars filled with peppernuts and tied with a simple red or green ribbon make lovely gifts.

— *Jewel Showalter, Landisville, PA*

Showalter Peppernuts

1½ cups shortening	1½ tsp. baking soda
3 cups sugar	1 tsp. each of cinnamon,
3 eggs	allspice, nutmeg,
1 cup dark corn syrup	ginger, cloves
¼ tsp. anise oil or	11 cups flour
1½ tsp. anise flavoring	
1 cup sour cream	
or buttermilk	

1. Cream shortening and sugar together. Add eggs and beat well.

2. Add corn syrup and anise.
3. Stir together all dry ingredients.
4. Add alternately with sour cream or buttermilk to creamed mixture.
5. When well blended, chill dough.
6. Form into rolls the size of a finger. Cut in pieces about the size of marbles.
7. Bake at 375° for 10 minutes.

This dough keeps well in the refrigerator so you can bake peppernuts throughout the season.
For a great post-meal ice-breaker, children can toss the peppernuts into the air and try to catch them in their mouths!
Fill everyone's pockets with peppernuts when you go out caroling!

— Jewel Showalter, Landisville, PA

★ Our children have entertained themselves and delighted us in creative ways as they "dress up" gingerbread people—another favorite of Christmas baking.

Michael, Lena, Lowell, and Miriam Brown
Grantham, PA

★ Out of our Swiss background come Springerle Cookies. Sugar Plum Loaves also have been a Christmas tradition in our family for many years. We often give them as gifts, and usually serve them for Christmas breakfast. A festive bread! Berliner Kranz cookies are another favorite during the holidays.

—*James and Helen Reusser, Kitchener, Ontario*

Springerle Cookies
Makes 3 dozen cookies

4 eggs   **4 drops oil of anise**
2 cups sugar   **4½ cups cake flour, sifted**

1. Beat eggs until thick. Gradually add sugar, beating well after each addition.
2. When all sugar has been added, beat 15 minutes with electric mixer or 30 minutes by hand.
3. Blend in anise oil. Fold in flour lightly, adding enough to be able to roll it with a cloth-covered rolling pin.
4. Roll ¼" thick on lightly floured board. Impress "pictures" on the dough with floured Springerle rolling pin or Springerle blocks. Cut cookies along the imprinted edges. Place on buttered cookie sheets. Allow to dry overnight.
5. Bake 30 minutes at 300°.
6. Store for a month in a covered jar with an orange or apple.

Sugar Plum Loaves
Makes 2 loaves

2 tsp. dry yeast
$\frac{1}{2}$ cup water (110°)
2 tsp. sugar
$\frac{3}{4}$ cup milk, scalded
$\frac{1}{2}$ cup sugar
$\frac{1}{4}$ cup shortening
$1\frac{1}{2}$ tsp. salt
$4\frac{3}{4}$-$5\frac{1}{4}$ cups all-purpose
   flour, sifted

1 tsp. grated lemon peel
2 beaten eggs
$1\frac{1}{2}$ cups mixed candied
   fruits and peels
confectioner's icing
nuts and candied
   cherry halves

1. Stir yeast into water. Add 2 tsp. sugar and allow yeast to become active (about 10 minutes).

2. Combine milk, $\frac{1}{2}$ cup sugar, shortening, and salt. Cool to lukewarm.

3. Add about 2 cups flour and the lemon peel. Beat until smooth.

4. Add eggs and beat well.

5. Stir in yeast mixture. Add fruits and peels. Stir in enough flour to make a soft dough.

6. Cover and let rest for 10 minutes.

7. Knead on lightly floured surface until smooth and elastic (6-8 minutes). Place in lightly greased bowl, turning once to grease surface.

8. Cover. Let rise till double (about $1\frac{1}{2}$-2 hours).

9. Punch down. Divide dough in half. Round each half into a ball. Cover and let rest 10 minutes.

10. Pat balls of dough into two round loaves. Place on greased cookie sheet. Pat tops to flatten slightly. Cover and let rise till double (about $1\frac{1}{2}$ hours).

11. Bake at 350° about 30 minutes. (Cover tops with foil after about 25 minutes to prevent over-browning.) Cool.

12. While still slightly warm, frost with confectioner's icing and decorate with nuts and candied cherry halves.

Berliner Kranz Cookies

³/₄ cup butter	2 cups flour, sifted
¹/₂ cup + 2 Tbsp.	¹/₄ tsp. salt
granulated sugar	1 egg white
1 tsp. grated orange peel	green sugar
1 egg	red cinnamon candies

1. Cream butter. Add ¹/₂ cup granulated sugar, orange peel, and egg. Beat until light.

2. Add flour and salt.

3. Chill for several hours, or until firm enough to roll.

4. Roll to ¹/₈" thickness. Cut out cookies with floured 2" doughnut cutter. Place on cookie sheets.

5. Beat egg white until foamy. Add 2 Tbsp. granulated sugar and beat until stiff. Brush cookies with this egg white mixture.

6. Decorate cookies with green sugar and cinnamon candies as follows: at three evenly separated areas of each cookie "wreath," sprinkle some green sugar to represent holly leaves. Then press three cinnamon candies into each area of "holly leaves" to represent the berries.

7. Bake at 400° 7-8 minutes. Remove to wire racks while hot.

★   After a big hearty turkey Christmas dinner, my family, through three generations, has served "Orange Charlotte"—a heavenly light dessert. This dessert has spread to Florida, Colorado, Washington, Virginia, and many other places, as nieces and nephews phone for Granny's Orange Charlotte recipe. They think it is just not Christmas without it.

—Ruth K. Nafziger, Bally, PA

Orange Charlotte

1 envelope unflavored gelatin	1 cup orange juice
1/3 cup cold water	1 Tbsp. lemon juice
1/3 cup hot water	2 egg whites, beaten until stiff
3/4 cup sugar	1/2 pint whipping cream

1. Dissolve gelatin in 1/3 cup cold water. Add 1/3 cup boiling water.
2. Add to this the sugar, orange juice, and lemon juice.
3. Place in refrigerator. When mixture begins to thicken, add beaten egg whites and cream.
4. Garnish with orange slices.

★ In our family Pecan Fingers (cookies) are a specialty and a tradition. My father, now in his 81st year, makes them himself, and his daughters, including me, make them in our homes. Somehow it just isn't Christmas without Pecan Fingers!

—*Gloria Lehman, Singers Glen, VA*

Pecan Fingers

1 cup real butter	2 cups flour
1/4 cup granulated sugar	1 cup pecans, chopped
1/4 tsp. salt	confectioner's sugar

1. Mix together butter, sugar, and salt.
2. Using your hands, mix in flour and pecans.
3. Form into finger shapes, making approximately 24 pieces.
4. Bake at 350° 25 minutes.
5. While hot, roll in confectioner's sugar.

Turnip Relish

5 lb. granulated sugar (11¼ cups)
1 qt. vinegar
1 fresh ginger root, shredded
4 lbs. turnips, cut in matchstick-size pieces
14-16 carrots, peeled and cut in matchstick-size pieces
½ cup salt
1 whole garlic, sliced
2 baskets small pearl onions, sliced
2 green bell peppers, cut in matchstick-size pieces
2 red bell peppers, cut in matchstick-size pieces

1. Boil together the sugar, vinegar, and ginger root until the sugar is completely dissolved, about 15 minutes. Set this syrup aside.
2. In large bowl toss together the turnips, carrots, and salt. Let mixture stand overnight.
3. In the morning, squeeze all liquid from above mixture.
4. Into sugar-vinegar syrup add garlic, onions, and green and red peppers.
5. Mix all ingredients together. Refrigerate until ready to serve.

★   Once a year I make a batch of Turnip Relish, which we know as "Christmas relish," to serve at our Christmas ham or turkey dinner, and to give as gifts.
—*Dawn Pichette, Harbor City, CA*

★   Oyster Filling is prepared by our family for every Christmas dinner and every Thanksgiving dinner!
—*Mary Jane Lederach Hershey, Harleysville, PA*

Oyster Filling

Serves 23 people as part of a holiday dinner.
(Never a morsel remains!)

24-oz. bag Trenton crackers
milk
3 doz. stewing (or larger)
   oysters, plus liquid

1½ sticks butter (12 Tbsp.)
coarse black pepper

1. Crack the Trenton crackers with a hammer. Place them in a large bowl.
2. Fill the bowl with milk and soak the crackers overnight.
3. In the morning, cut each oyster in half and mix all of them with the crackers. Add the oyster liquid.
4. Grease 2 Pyrex loaf dishes (either 9" x 5" x 3" or 10" x 5" x 3"). Divide mixture between the 2 dishes. Sprinkle the tops with coarse black pepper.
5. Cut the butter into long, thin slivers. Push the slivers down into the oyster mixture, starting at one end of each dish and continuing to the other end of each dish.
6. Bake at 375° for 1 hour, or until well browned and crusty on top.

★ I make Christmas Danish Swirls only once a year—for Christmas morning.Weeks before, I'm reminded that the family is expecting and anticipating them: "I can't wait to eat those Danish rolls Christmas morning."

We always eat oyster stew for Christmas Eve. This tradition started before my generation and continues, even though most of my family doesn't even like oysters! In the morning of Christmas Eve day, we put the oysters, milk, salt, pepper, and a little margarine or butter into the crockpot, set it on low, and let it cook all day. Throughout the day the lid is lifted for whiffs. The big round hard oyster crackers are part of the tradition. One doesn't have to eat oysters to enjoy them broken into the hot broth.

—*Sarah and Herb Myers, Mount Joy, PA*

Christmas Danish Swirls

2½-3 cups flour
½ cup sugar
1½ tsp. salt
2 Tbsp. cornstarch
2 tsp. grated lemon peel
2 Tbsp. yeast
¾ cup milk
½ cup water
¼ cup margarine

2 eggs (at room
   temperature), separated
1 cup whole wheat flour
1½ cups
   (3 sticks) margarine
1 Tbsp. water
confectioner's sugar
   frosting
red and green sprinkles

1. Mix 1 cup flour, sugar, salt, cornstarch, lemon peel, and undissolved yeast in a large bowl.

2. Combine milk, water, and ¼ cup margarine in a saucepan. Heat over low heat until liquids are warm. Gradually add to dry ingredients and beat 2 minutes, scraping bowl occasionally. Add 2 egg yolks, 1 egg white (reserve remaining egg white) and 1 cup whole wheat flour. Beat vigorously by hand or with electric mixer on high for 2 minutes, scraping bowl occasionally. Add enough additional flour to make a stiff batter; stir just until blended. Cover tightly with aluminum foil; chill about 1 hour.

3. Spread 1½ cups margarine into a 10" x 12" rectangle on waxed paper. Chill 1 hour.

4. Roll chilled dough into a 12" x 16" rectangle on a lightly floured surface. Place margarine slab on ⅔ of dough. Fold uncovered third over middle section; cover with remaining third. Give dough a quarter turn; roll into a 12" x 16" rectangle; fold as above. Turn, roll, and fold once more; chill 1 hour. Repeat procedure of two rollings, foldings, turnings, and chillings two more times. Then refrigerate overnight in a covered plastic container or floured plastic bag.

5. Divide dough in half. On a lightly floured board roll half the dough into a 15" x 6" rectangle. Cut 12 strips, 15" x ½". Twist each strip and form into a circle, sealing ends well. Place on greased baking sheets. Repeat with remaining piece of dough. Cover lightly with plastic wrap; refrigerate overnight.

6. Combine reserved egg white with 1 Tbsp. water. Brush rolls with egg white mixture.

7. Bake at 375° about 15 to 20 minutes, or until done. Remove from baking sheets and cool on wire racks. Frost with confectioner's sugar frosting and decorate with red and green sprinkles.

★   I like to make pumpkin/pecan pie because it is less rich than pecan pie.
— *Erma Wenger, Lancaster, PA*

Pumpkin Pecan Pie

3 eggs, slightly beaten
1 cup canned or
    cooked pumpkin
1 cup sugar
½ cup dark corn syrup

1 tsp. vanilla
½ tsp. cinnamon
¼ tsp. salt
1 pie shell, unbaked
1 cup chopped pecans

1. Combine first seven ingredients and pour into shell.
2. Sprinkle pecans on top.
3. Bake at 350° for 40 minutes or until knife inserted halfway between center and edge comes out clean.

★   We have a quince tree in our backyard. In September and October, I make many jars of beautiful golden jelly with its unique flavor. Many people seem to enjoy Christmas gifts of jelly.
— *Mary Ellen and Albert Meyer, Goshen, IN*

★   Grandma Jost (whose ancestors went from Holland to Prussia to Russia to Kansas and California) makes pepper-nuts. Aunt Kathie makes all-fruit fruitcake.
— *Ruth and Timothy Stoltzfus Jost, Columbus, OH*

★   Raisin Nut Bread is an ideal food to give to neighbors, the mail carrier, your doctor, etc. I bake a loaf, slip it into a plastic baggy, wrap it in colorful paper or cellophane wrap, and top it with a pretty bow. The tradition has been picked up by our married daughter, and now she also bakes the little Christmas breads to give to her friends.
— *Esther and Dave Kniss, Gulfport, MS*

Raisin Nut Bread

2 cups raisins
2 cups water
2 tsp. baking soda
2 eggs
1½ cups sugar

1 tsp. vanilla
dash of salt
3 cups sifted flour
1 cup chopped nuts

1. Combine raisins, water, and soda. Bring to a boil. When mixture begins to foam, remove from heat and cool.
2. Beat together eggs, sugar, vanilla, and salt.
3. Add raisin mixture alternately with flour to the egg mixture. Fold in nuts.
4. Pour batter into 4 or 5 well greased and floured #2 cans and bake at 350° for 1 hour.

★ I make a double batch of gingerbread cookie dough, and then gather a good variety of small candies, dried fruits, nuts for decorations, and a large assortment of cookie cutters. My children invite a couple of friends home, and we have a big cookie-making party. There's lots of opportunity for creative expressions and lots of good eating and sharing!

—Margaret, Samuel, Bart, and Hannah
Wenger Johnson, Keezletown, VA

Chocolate-Dipped Apricots

Melt ½ **cup chocolate chips** in microwave oven at 50% power (or melt over double boiler). Stir in **1 Tbsp. shortening.** Dip each **dried apricot** in the chocolate until half of apricot is covered. Let cool on waxed paper. This is great to do with small helpers! Even 2-year-olds can manage.

—Ann and Byron Weber Becker
Kitchener, Ontario

Potato Candy

1 small potato, peeled and cooked
confectioner's sugar
peanut butter

1. Mash the potato in a 1-quart bowl. Add confectioner's sugar until mixture is of the consistency of pie dough.
2. Roll dough out on waxed paper to the thickness of pie dough.
3. Shape into a rectangle. Spread with thin layer of peanut butter.
4. Roll up from one long side and then cut slices ¼" thick.
— *Twila and Mark Taylor, Baltimore, MD*

★ My mother and her brother had a special way to eat chocolate drops and peanuts. After each bite (or nibble) of chocolate, they plastered the exposed white portion with peanut halves. It makes a good combination.
— *E. Elaine Kauffman, Campinas, SP, Brazil*

★ Our friend makes the usual Christmas cookies each year. She puts them on a plate with ribbon and then hand-delivers them to friends, the sick, and elderly. Not only do we receive cookies, but we get a real visit from our dear friend.
— *Joyce Eigsti Hofer, Denver, CO*

3.
Ideas and Traditions for Advent

> *"Each successive night*
> *we stealthily deliver*
> *our little gifts.*
> *It takes creativity to deliver*
> *without being discovered!*
> *We love it."*

Note: There are many ideas for Advent in the two earlier chapters. Here are additional ones.

★ Our Christmas Chain, made with 25 red and green construction paper loops, is a visual way to count down the days till Christmas. Each day we tear off a loop of the chain. Some years, when our daughters were younger, it helped to remind us of happenings. Written on the chains would be such things as: this evening we will go caroling; today is Uncle Dan's birthday; Grandpa and Grandma arrive tomorrow; Daddy is off work today; last day of school in 199?; we have tickets for *The Nutcracker* tonight.

This year on the green chains were written things to thank God for (health, food, friends, God's word, water, seasons, air to breathe, books, laughter). On the red chains were immediate and extended family members to pray for.

Our Advent calendar is a banner made of natural felt. A green felt tree fills most of the upper two-thirds of the banner with 24 pieces of Velcro attached to the tree and one under the tree beside the trunk.

Three rows of red felt numbered pockets, made with strips of burlap divided by stitching, fill the bottom one-third of the banner. In each pocket is a scripture verse and a small something, wrapped in tissue paper, that relates to the verse.

In the first row are things associated with Christmas (like snow, song, laughter, joy, children); the second row relates to who Jesus is (the way, the light, the door, the bread of life); and the final row includes the main characters and events in the Christmas story. All of these objects can be stuck onto the tree.

After using those objects for many years, we made small counted-cross-stitched chrismons to attach to the tree instead. For years we alternated between using the original objects and the chrismons. More recently we have used a Jesse Tree banner.

—Sarach and Herb Myers, Mount Joy, PA

★ Our Advent observances are quite simple. Shortly after Thanksgiving, we purchase a number of poinsettias for the living room and dining room. These are the only decorations we put up until just before Christmas.

We deliberately refrain from playing Christmas music and from eating Christmas goodies until Christmas has nearly arrived. In this way we fully anticipate the festival of Christmas.

At dinner each evening during advent we light our Advent candle and read aloud the Christmas cards and letters which have arrived in that day's mail.

We often participate in an Advent prayer retreat early in the season.

—Marlene and Stanley Kropf, Elkhart, IN

★ We've started a new tradition—the 12 days of Christmas. Twelve days before Christmas, we take a small gift to our chosen family (perhaps a neighbor—a new family at church—someone ill). We secretly set the gift, decorated with a bow, on their porch.

Then the next night, we put two small items, each with a bow, at the same spot. The third night we take three. Each successive night we stealthily deliver our little gifts. It takes creativity to deliver without being discovered! We love it.

On Christmas Eve we take our last gift and sing "The 12 Days of Christmas," putting our items into the song, thus revealing ourselves. (For example, "On the first day of Christmas my true love gave to me—a pumpkin with a shiny green bow," or "On the second day of Christmas my true love gave to me—two bright red candles.")

—*David and Martha Clymer family, Shirleysburg, PA*

★ This year was very different. In a shopping mall I dropped a coin into the Salvation Army pot, and, without expecting it, the woman ringing the bell at the pot gave me a tiny "blessing card." I popped it open when I got home, and it read: "Consecrate yourselves, for tomorrow the Lord will do amazing things among you." (Joshua 3:5) Maybe it spoke to me because I had a worrisome (big) meeting to lead. But the promise didn't just help for the meeting—it took me all through Christmas. It still gives me a very warm feeling. More people should receive such an unexpected gift. It's wonderful!

—*Peter and Susan Kehler, Sumas, WA*

★ My sister always sent calendars to our grandchildren. She died recently. I will carry on that tradition.

—*Arlene Egli, Goshen, IN*

★ It has been the practice of Filipino families to go to church at dawn, beginning on December 16, to sing and celebrate the coming of the Messiah. On the way back home, they buy a rice cake, specially made for the occasion. We call the rice cake "puto bumbong." "Puto" is a ground rice. "Bumbong" is a bamboo tube. The puto is put in a bamboo tube and then steamed. It is really a time for family fellowship.

The night before Christmas, families gather together and patch up differences or misunderstandings that have occurred during the year, so that together they will face the new year as new and pure, without blemish. They start the year anew.

—*Luis A. Lumibao, San Jose City, Philippines*

★ This year, we started Advent by making wreath cookies, symbolizing the never-ending love of Jesus. Use any cut-out cookie dough; color half of it green and leave the other half white. Roll out one tablespoon of each color of dough as long and wide as a pencil. Twist them together like a rope, and shape the twist into a wreath.

We invited another family to help us make wreath cookies, and then gave them to children at church on the first Sunday in Advent.

One year I started Advent with a day of silent retreat. Our meditation was guided into thinking about Jesus' coming to us, and what a difference that makes in our lives. That year was the most peace-filled preparation for Christmas I've ever had. Even in my busyness, I felt more focused on Jesus, and more deliberate about what I had to do or not do.

—Sandra and John Drescher-Lehman, Richmond, VA

★ During our infant son's first year, we took him to the hospital one evening to await open-heart surgery the following day. That night we came home to a dark, cold house, unadorned by even the usual Advent wreath. Then we could share with Mary some of the bittersweet meaning of that first Christmas, when "Mary pondered all these things."

—Marj and Delbert Wiens, Fresno, CA

> ## *"The aim was to see how full and soft we could make the cradle before Christmas Eve."*

★ Instead of an Advent wreath, we have used a log (slab of wood), into which we placed candles, and then read the appropriate scriptures each of the weeks of Advent. (Holes had been driven into the wood to accommodate candles.)

—*Richard and Betty Pellman, Millersville, PA*

★ On the first Sunday of Advent, we usually attend the multi-generational event/workshop held at our church. There are crafts of all kinds—mostly making small gifts or decorations, cookie baking, candy making, story telling, etc. Leaders of projects furnish supplies, and participants go to whichever station interests them.

After a light supper (furnished by the church), we all gather in the sanctuary for a short Advent service and the lighting of the first candle. Later on at home, we make our own Advent wreath from greenery we've collected before and have our own short service.

—*Grace and Werner Will, Stevensville, MT*

★ Beginning with the first Sunday of Advent, we start singing Advent Christmas songs, usually in the evening before the children go to bed. We have a calendar with 24 bags. The bags are numbered, and each day of December the children open one bag in the morning. The bags contain candy, cookie cutters, Christmas ornaments, etc.

—*Barry, Erika, Karina, and Anya Kreider*
Halle, Germany

★ One year we had a *posadas* party, a Central American tradition, acting out Mary and Joseph going to different homes looking for lodging, ending with a party and a piñata for adults and kids.

Another year we had a baby shower for Jesus in early December; gifts (used clothes, new toys, baby supplies) were donated to a local food and clothes closet.

— Cindy Bryant Weidman, Richmond, VA

★ We can trace our family history by referring to the different Advent wreaths and crèches that have enhanced our celebration of Christmas. Lighting the Advent candles every breakfast has remained our tradition, even though only my husband and I enjoy their light now.

—Justina M. Heese, Steinbach, Manitoba

★ A "*Good Housekeeping* Story" began an Advent tradition in our family. We kept a copy of the story, "The Last Straw," and always read it on the first Sunday of Advent.

Then we put the names of the family in a bowl, and each person drew one. We put the small cradle, made for Grandma when she was two, in a prominent place, close to where the manger scene was set up. We placed a bag of straw close beside it.

For the next week we did kind deeds for the person whose name we had drawn, without revealing our identity. For each deed accomplished, we placed straw in the little cradle.

The following Sunday, we again placed the names in the bowl, and again we each drew one. The aim was to see how full and soft we could make the cradle before Christmas Eve. We learned many lessons from that exercise and had a lot of fun and satisfaction from thinking of someone else's happiness.

—Norman and Ruth Smith, Ailsa Cruig, Ontario

★ In our congregation, each new family is given a yule log on the first Sunday of Advent. Each year we pull ours out of storage and use it first at the Advent soup supper which closes with candle-lighting. We use it each time during Advent when we do devotion time. We find candles help us to center ourselves.
—Stan, Carol, Sarah, and Ben Miller Histand
Soldotna, AK

★ Although we are now only two again, we think it important to keep the family Advent traditions which we initiated when our children were preschoolers. We seasonize our home, beginning with the first Sunday in Advent through Epiphany. Each Sunday evening (or Monday if Sunday hasn't allowed enough hours) we light the appropriate candle, read one of the day's lectionary passages, sing a verse of "O Come, O Come, Emmanuel," and pray in quiet silence as we gather round the Advent wreath which has been garnished with fresh greens on a purple cloth.
—Alice and Willard Roth, Elkhart, IN

★ Al and I spent our first three married years in Europe and enjoyed one Christmas with German friends in the Black Forest. There I saw my first Advent wreath—a simple fresh pine wreath with four red candles and four red bows. We have made our own each year since. We have often have a cranberry-based hot punch and early Christmas cookies with each reading of the Advent scriptures.
—Mary Ellen and Albert Meyer, Goshen, IN

★ Through the years, I've read various Christmas classics aloud to the children.
—Chester and Sara Jane Wenger, Lancaster, PA

★ We attend a local church's Lessons and Carols service with a group of friends, then meet for dinner afterwards.
—Keith and Gail Pentz, Casselberry, FL

★ We put up a felt tree banner on December 1st. Every day we add an "ornament" with a symbol on the front and a Bible verse on the back. It starts with Old Testament prophecies and goes on to the New Testament and Revelation.

—*Kym Sutter, Manson, IA*

★ We have always made a small fuss about St. Nicholas Day. The children put their shoes outside their doors on the night of December 5—and find small gifts in them in the morning. We have never encouraged belief in Santa Claus, but instead have tried to tell St. Nicholas's story.

We also try to make a fuss at Epiphany, January 6, with a couple of presents (usually ones that were misplaced or didn't arrive by Christmas) and some attention to the story of the Magi.

We don't put up decorations until (at least) the first Sunday of Advent (the neighbors always do it Thanksgiving Day)—but leave them up until Epiphany, trying to show that our lives are based on the "Christmas calendar."

We light Advent wreath candles at dinner each night and take turns reading from an Advent devotional booklet. We found putting greens in a large, shallow bowl filled with sand allowed us to water them over the six weeks. Also, if you put candles in the freezer, they burn more slowly—so the one from the first Sunday can last until Christmas.

— The Baker-Smiths, Waitsburg, WA

★ Every year my mother prepared an Advent candle for our family and several others to give to friends and extended family. The tall white candles had the numbers 1-25 painted in red, and green holly decorations. Beginning December 1, we burned down through the numbers, day by day, until Christmas arrived. As children, we loved watching the candle burn and blowing it out at the precise moment. As adults, we enjoy passing on the tradition.

—Karen Miller Rush, Harrisonburg, VA

★ For several years now, we have celebrated each Sunday of Advent. We light the appropriate candle on the wreath, plus a few other candles in the living room, sit on the floor in the semi-darkness, sing "O Come, O Come, Emmanuel," and then Mom reads some Christmas-related or inspirational story. It is often a time to talk more about what happened in worship that morning.

—Jim, Lois, Britt, Austin, Reid, and Lane
Kaufmann, New Paris, IN

> *"It is an awesome thing*
> *to wake from sleep*
> *to this*
> *heavenly music."*

★ Part of the anticipation of Christmas is getting cards and letters from friends and relatives. We wait to open the Christmas messages until the end of the day, when we can enjoy them together.

—*Joyce Eigsti Hofer, Denver, CO*

★ My daughter had her children open a small gift each day beginning December 1. It was always something related to Christ's birth or the Bible.

—*Miriam Shoup, Orrville, OH*

★ As the Christmas holidays approached, we told our children that Christmas is celebrated in two ways. The most important is the birth of Christ. The other is a folk festival—trees, gifts, cookies.

—*Ellen and Paul Peachey, Harpers Ferry, WV*

★ Our Advent season opens with a special event. At midnight before the first Advent Sunday, our youth group walks through the apartment houses of our community, singing Christmas hymns. They often leave an Advent calendar, a candle, or a set of cards with each household. It is an awesome thing to wake from sleep to this heavenly music.

—*David and Louisa Mow, Farmington, PA*

★ We start on the first Sunday of Advent, lighting the first candle on our candle board. (We have found it very useful to use the Advent weekly worship service, found in *Why Not Celebrate* by Sara Wenger Shenk.) At the same time we start setting up the crèche; every day that we are able to have a service, someone brings a new piece to the stable. It is slowly assembled. On Christmas Day we add the baby. Sometimes we like to continue till Kings Day, having the Kings arrive. We take turns, someone lighting the candle, another blowing it out, the next bringing a piece to the stable, and someone else helping with the reading.

— Becky Wigginton, Chaco, Argentina

★ When our children were young, their grandmother sent a different Advent calendar each year.

— LaVerna Klippenstein, Winnipeg, Manitoba

★ My wife, who is an elementary school principal, was asked to speak about Christmas in Turkey (where we traveled last summer). She pointed out to the third grade classes she addressed that Turkey is a Muslim country and does not really celebrate Christmas. However, she used the occasion to speak about St. Nicholas who lived in what is now Turkey. From there the idea of Santa Claus eventually emerged. So she gave the children a lesson in church history and traditions.

— Carl Jantzen, Seven Mile, OH

★ Our family celebrates Advent using a unique calendar. I received this as a gift from a special aunt and it includes a wooden Christmas ornament behind each door. We attach the ornaments to a garland hung above an archway in our family room.

— Connie Faber, Hillsboro, KS

★ After Thanksgiving Day, we each take 25 slips of paper. We each write prayer requests on the papers and place them in a basket near the dining room. Starting on December 1, each morning we individually remove a prayer request. Each person is responsible to pray for that concern throughout the day. We decided as a family to keep the prayer requests confidential within the family.

> —*Dennis, Sharon, Daniel, and Heather Showalter*
> *West Liberty, OH*

★ When the children were young, I always read "Twas the Night Before Christmas" by Clement Clarke Moore, and my husband prepared a Bible devotional appropriate to the children's ages.

> —*Faye Nyce, Grantham, PA*

★ Because our family consists of four people, we are able to focus on one individual each week during Advent. After the reading and singing, we discuss that person's year—successes, disappointments, areas of growth, changes. We conclude with each of us praying for the person of the week.

> —*Steve and Phyllis Swartz, London, OH*

★ We put candies under the children's pillows to remind them of the coming gift of Christ.

> —*Fred and Margaret Heese, Wymark, Saskatchewan*

> *"Amazingly,*
> *we all look forward*
> *to our*
> *candlelight suppers."*

★ I write a Christmas letter in which I review the past year and once again connect with friends overseas, as well as in the U. S. and Canada.

— *Eugene and Gladys Sprunger, Berne, IN*

★ We decided to ask our very small, oldest child (while the others were still too young to communicate) his thoughts and feelings about replacing the traditional tree "bobbles" with simpler, more durable ornaments that had been made by poor artisans in places/industries overseas.

Each year at our church's annual Self-Help sale, he (and later his brothers and sister) and my wife and I chose one or two ornaments as a personal way of contributing to the creator's family (and, of course, to our tree). Now our children insist that this is their way!

— *Ben and Clare Neufeld, Delta, British Columbia*

★ Every evening during Advent and Epiphany, we eat supper by candlelight—each child chooses their own candleholder (made by their great-grandfather) and candle—all of which we place on a cloth in the center of the table.

After the candles are lit, we tell or read a story, sing a song, say a choral reading, or read from the Bible one of the interesting stories of how God worked with his people in the Old Testament.

For each story I have made a symbol (with Velcro on the back) which we place on our Jesse Tree banner each evening. For example—a rainbow for the story of Noah, a harp for David, a trumpet for the walls of Jericho, a sheaf of wheat for Ruth and Naomi, a kneading bread bowl for the Exodus, etc. We got the idea for our Jesse Tree from a book which we have since lost—so each year we make some different symbols to go with some different Old Testament stories. Our stories culminate with the birth of Jesus on December 24.

After our celebration of the Jesse Tree, we eat supper. We finish off by opening another window on our Advent calendar. Then the children blow out their respective candles.

Amazingly, we all look forward to our candlelight suppers, retelling stories of God's actions with His people, and opening the Advent calendar windows. Often our candles keep lighting our supper tables on into January!

—*Helen Stoltzfus Bowman, Millersburg, IN*

4.
Music Ideas and Traditions

★ One of our traditions usually happens in November or early December. When it snows for the first time, we take that as the signal to play Christmas music, but only for that day. We wait until the middle of December to begin playing Christmas music regularly.

—*Jim, Lois, Britt, Austin, Reid, and Lane Kaufmann*
New Paris, IN

> *"I received my mother's*
> *leather-bound* Messiah *score*
> *on the last Christmas*
> *of her life."*

★ We started singing "The Friendly Beast" song when our children were quite small, and it's still a favorite after six or seven years. Each one of us takes the part of one of the animals and sings that part. (I have always been the camel, and each of the children have their own special animals they always ask to sing.) A few years back I made donkey ears for the donkey to wear, curly horns for the sheep, and ears and horns for the cow; even a beak and shining eyes for the rooster. Those were a big hit!
—*Becky Wigginton, Chaco, Argentina*

★ A few days before Christmas, we invite friends to our home for a Christmas carol sing. We sing old and new carols, and each year our family of four prepares and sings one or two special numbers. After the singing, we feast on a rich array of special foods—including Stan's English cucumber sandwiches, spicy meatballs, Christmas cookies and breads, candies, and cheesecake.
—*Marlene and Stanley Kropf, Elkhart, IN*

★ I know one family who sends music to each other—so they can practice on their own, like piano duets, quartets, etc.—then when they get together, they play and sing what they have practiced—and they surprise each other by how wonderfully it turns out.
—*Alice Buehler, Elmira, Ontario*

★ The local farm museum has an annual program which includes a sing-along around a campfire. Many people carry old oil lamps or punched tin candle lights. The old-fashioned toys under a Victorian Christmas tree, homemade cookies, and hot mulled cider create an awe about Christmas past, and a memorable evening.

—*Erma Wenger, Lancaster, PA*

★   The day after Halloween, we start playing Christmas music. We play baroque, ancient music like Gregorian chants. After that, we play music that sounds more like Christmas.

—*Dale and Rosie Horst, Newton, KS*

> *"Each one of us takes the part of one of the animals and sings that part."*

★   Everett and I enjoy supporting choirs at our workplaces which sing at Christmas time. Everett works for a German company. Every Christmas, his choir participates in a German Christmas service at a Lutheran church in down-town Pittsburgh with the complete service in German.

—*Leona Kraybill Myer, Pittsburgh, PA*

★   I grew up as a professor's kid. *The Messiah* was per-formed in our college community every December. As a child, I was allowed to pick out one gift to open on "Messiah Sunday." My mother always sang in the large community chorus—37 years, until lung cancer took her life. I first started singing in the community chorus when I was 15.

I received my mother's leather-bound *Messiah* score on the last Christmas of her life. I used that score as her voice when I was invited to sing the soprano solos that last

Christmas. She was not able to attend the performance, but I knew her spirit and joy for singing carried my voice to the high B flat in the closing phrase.

Our family has carried on the tradition of listening to and singing in *The Messiah*. When possible, we've also been involved in many musical traditions from around the world through international service experiences.

— Elizabeth Raid Pankratz, Newton, KS

★ We carol with a group of church members and go house to house, singing. Early in the morning of the 25th, we listen to recorded music and songs.

— Thabitha, Daniel R. John Sankararto, Mary S.
Rao, Mr. and Mrs. Ron Peters, Gadwal, India

★ When I was growing up, we went to see *Amahl and the Night Visitors* almost every year. We went to Philadelphia where my great-aunt and great-grandmother lived. From their house we would take the train downtown and see the musical performed in a cathedral. My aunt and grandmother no longer live in Philadelphia, but I still try to see the play every year. I know it by memory, but I still love to see it.

— Cindy Horning, Denver, PA

★ The year we had a baby on December 8, the only "Christmas" thing I did was to go to a performance of *The Messiah*. Since then, if I hear, or preferably help to sing, this piece of music, my Christmas is complete.

—Sandra and John Drescher-Lehman, Richmond, VA

★ Starting in the fall, we sing Christmas carols as we all lie quietly tucked in our beds. We may continue this into January.

—*Dorcas Breckbill, Newmanstown, PA*

★ Caroling for other people is one of the best parts of Christmas. Children can learn the names of elderly church members whom they rarely see, and they can experience the joy and thankfulness these people share. This is also a good way for children to learn to sing Christmas songs and to memorize them. It's a wonderful *giving* experience because one *gets* so much in return.

—*Roy and Loretta Kaufman, Sterling, IL*

★ I am so grateful that my parents encouraged us children to attend the annual performance of Handel's *The Messiah* in the great Massey Hall in Toronto. When I started to go out with a boyfriend (whom I later married), one of our first dates was to be to this performance. He got the mumps and I missed my first concert in years. But we did attend together for a number of years after that, until church service took us out of the country.

When we lived in India we missed the caroling, yet we came to enjoy being part of the special and enthusiastic celebration among the Christians of our area and the Bihar Province. Groups traveled from village to village, singing and playing musical instruments as they went. By the time they reached a village, a crowd had gathered, and they told the story of Jesus, from birth to death to resurrection. On the final night, all touring groups converged at a central location, singing, dancing and praising, a truly culturally relevant means of celebrating the birth of Jesus.

We now live at a retirement community in Pennsylvania, and we are thrilled with the carol tradition practiced here. One of the apartment complexes has balconies on four levels, overlooking a central atrium. Everything is gorgeously decorated with the usual tree, lots of poinsettias, and garlands.

On an evening before Christmas, residents and friends gather on all levels. On each floor is a song leader, working in harmonony with one major director. Carols are sung up and down, back and forth, floor by floor, or by whatever creative pattern the director calls for. The evening concludes with punch and lots of Christmas cookies made by the residents. A beautiful evening to remember and a sharp contrast to Christmas in India—yet culturally relevant for this place.

—*Erma J. Sider, Mechanicsburg, PA*

★ Some years we learn a new Christmas song during Advent, singing it every evening at supper-time.

—*Rod and Martha Yoder Mast, Indianapolis, IN*

★ For twenty-some years, on the weekend before Christmas (usually on a Friday evening), we had a community caroling party. We purchased a set of about 30 books of carols, and sang from these books, year after year.

Our farmhouse had a large living room. Everyone sat in a big circle and selected carols to sing. As the children grew, the singing became more robust and harmonious. And always a child read the Christmas story from Luke. Many times a child did a recitation which had been prepared for a school program. Some years children brought instruments and played. One year we did a Christmas skit with the children dressed as angels. And without exception, everyone consumed the anticipated cookies and punch.

To this day, the memories of these warm, pre-Christmas gatherings bring special feelings of joy. And throughout the year, as I unexpectedly meet neighbors and their children, they remind me about those long past evenings of fellowship.

—*Mary Jane Lederach Hershey, Hurleysville, PA*

★ Normally, the townsfolk gather at the square or plaza to hear a special kind of music written for the occasion. We usually have a singing competition, and the winner is given a cash prize and his/her song is recorded.

There is caroling, also, but the government only gives a permit to cause-oriented groups, such as if the proceeds from the caroling will go to a charitable institution, or to less fortunate children, like the street kids.

—Luis A. Lumibao, San Jose City, Philippines

★ Family singing is livened up when we give the children small percussion instruments such as bells, triangles, or toy drums. "Willie Bring Your Little Drum" is a great delight.

—David and Louisa Mow, Farmington, PA

★ I am a music teacher so I have my students give their annual Christmas recital in our church, the first or second Saturday in December. The church is always filled. Parents bring snack foods for the reception which follows. I just had my 35th recital.

—Faye and Harry Pankratz, Inola, OR

★ We share and exchange cassettes, or loan one to friends, singing along, learning new songs. If we feel the spirit nudge at our "heartstrings," we make some comments about the lyrics.

—Charles and Lisa Christano, Kudus, Indonesia

> ## "My father sang 'Silent Night,' to a string quartet and piano in German; then one of our friends sang it in Japanese."

★ One year, our string-playing children and friends, as well as my parents, were spending Christmas with us. My father sang "Silent Night," to a string quartet and piano in German; then one of our friends sang it in Japanese. Finally we all sang it in English and German, while our friend sang it in Japanese in a perfect soprano obligato. My parents are gone now, but we play that recording frequently at Christmas and re-create the "high" it gave us.
—*John and Betty Wittrig, Winfield, IA*

★ Our family members all sing together lustily before gift time. Although we have some song sheets, everyone knows the verses by memory because I used to pay them a nickel for each verse that they could recite and sing. We also have a mini-recital by anyone who is currently practicing an instrument—sort of a family orchestra.
—*Hilda J. Born, Abbotsford, British Columbia*

★ This Christmas, at my brother's home, I awoke to the same little tune, "Wake happy children, on this Christmas morn," that I heard for years in my parents' home, and which I've played for my own children.
—*Marj and Delbert Wiens, Fresno, CA*

★ Our small church fellowship keeps the caroling tradition alive by singing to many of our neighbors within a two-mile distance of the church. It is a highlight for the children, and many of our "guests" say they *used* to go caroling, or they *used* to get carolers. So it is fun to be a carrier of music, as well as of loaves of bread for each household we sing to.
—*Grace Nolt, Canadensis, PA*

★ We enjoy our community carol sing in the park, gathered around a bonfire with hot chocolate and cookies afterwards.
— *Carol and Jim Spicher, Mountville, PA*

★ My husband does a lot of performing during Advent. He plays solo autoharp and is often hired to stroll at gatherings while playing Christmas carols. While this can make the month of December feel extra busy, it also provides us with the side benefit of having live music throughout the month while Les practices.

Throughout the year I sing our children to sleep. During Advent I make an effort to sing Christmas songs. Our three-year-old son often asks for a new song, so I keep a hymnal by the bed for easy referral.
— *Gwen Gustafson-Zook, Portland, OR*

★ For about three or four years, I sent out a "Let's get together and sing carols" invitation to all the people on our block. Approximately 30 people gathered for a Sunday night sing-along. One neighbor who had musical training played our old organ and directed. Some of the teenagers came, too. It was a very festive evening.
— *Sarah Yoder Scott, Newark, DE*

★ I play carols on the piano after the children are in bed, and they like that.

— *The Stoner family, Fredericksburg, PA*

★ Our family has a tradition of taking cookies to and singing for our neighbors. At certain ages the children growled or grumbled about it. As they got older, they like it once again.

— *David and Martha Clymer family*
Shirleysburg, PA

★ We start Christmas carols on November 28th. This dates back to a special occasion when our oldest children were small. It all began with a walk during a beautiful snowfall on that date.

— *Fred and Margaret Heese, Wymark, Saskatchewan*

★ The best gift we found to give our 92-year-old grandma, whose needs are minimal and who lives at a retirement home, is to surprise her some evening in December with caroling. Then we all move to a fellowship hall for finger-food snacks we've brought along.

— *Jan Steffy Mast, Lancaster, PA*

★ I usually listen to *The Messiah* while addressing Christmas cards.

— *Mary Lahman Heatwole, Harrisonburg, VA*

> *"I play carols
> on the piano
> after the children
> are in bed."*

★   When our family is ready to put up the tree, and all the decorations are out, we play *The Messiah* to put us in a spirit of anticipating the season. We enjoy the music and sing along as we trim the tree together.

> —*Elaine Lepp Karber, Long Beach, CA*

★   During coffee hour between Sunday School and church throughout the month of December, there is a sing-along of Christmas carols around the piano in the church parlor.

> —*Grace and Werner Will, Stevensville, MT*

5.

Ideas and Traditions for Giving and Receiving Gifts

★ This year my three-year-old son, Si, was part of our family's first-ever cousin gift exchange (the adults have been exchanging names for years). Each child was responsible for getting a gift for another child.

After an unfruitful visit to the neighborhood toy store, Si and I decided to make a cookie-baking kit for four-year-old Leah. Si and I then made three packages of master oatmeal cookie baking mix (one with mini M&Ms, one with cinnamon and raisins, and one with coconut).

Next, we went to a fabric store and Si picked out fabric which "we" made into a small apron. We also took a trip to a discount store where Si got a small cookie sheet, a hot mitt, and a small wooden spoon.

We packaged it all up in a one-gallon ice cream bucket, covered with contact paper. Si was enthusiastic and very involved throughout the whole process.

When he presented Leah with her packages, Si was as excited about giving a gift as he was about receiving one. He was obviously proud to be sharing something he had made especially for Leah. Leah loved her cookie-baking kit. She immediately put on her apron and wanted to get started.

— Gwen Gustafson-Zook, Portland, OR

★ Through the years we have continued to fill stockings— for adults and children. This remains a highlight of Christmas get-togethers. Filling stockings takes less work and money than buying presents for everyone. The practice can reflect a lot of creativity, too.

One creative mother in our church has found a solution to children peeking at gifts under the tree to see who they are for. She writes the names of the persons who are to receive the gifts in code. In the days before Christmas, the children enjoy trying to crack the code.

— Karen Miller Rush, Harrisonburg, VA

★ The last several years I have pieced a comforter for each of our four children's families before Thanksgiving. On our Thanksgiving Day family get-together, we knot these and then each family has a comforter to give to someone at Christmas-time.

I am always surprised at the diverse ways they choose to give the comforters. Our grandchildren are old enough now that they can help with the knotting and with the decision of who should receive them. Some recipients have been a homeless man, living between two buildings in Wichita; a foster boy, eight years old, who now had a new blanket to take along when he was adopted; a first grade friend of one grandchild, who didn't have a blanket to keep warm at night.
— *Ben and Lorraine Myers, Dillsburg, PA*

★ In our immediate family, all kinds of things got wrapped, often creatively as animals, birds, etc. Underwear, used items from the thrift shop, and coupons for dishwashing or other services were in the huge stack, along with the "real" gifts. It took all morning to unwrap them one by one. A favorite laugh-getter was the score card from a previous family game, presented by the winner to the loser.
— *James and Anna Juhnke, North Newton, KS*

> ## *"Instead of giving gifts to each other, we give nativity sets to our friends."*

★ I have made it a tradition to choose one book each Christmas for each family member. I write a special message for the person inside the book, along with the recipient's name and the year. Now that our children are grown, they have continued this tradition by giving Everett and me books. It's fun to see what they choose for us!

—*Leona Kraybill Myer, Pittsburgh, PA*

★ One family has a unique way of gift-giving. Instead of giving gifts to each other, we give nativity sets to our friends. One part of the scene is delivered each evening by a carrier for the five days prior to Christmas Day.

The first day the stable or shelter is delivered to the home of the recipient. This is followed by the shepherds, then Mary and Joseph beside an empty manger, and later the wise men.

We wrap each gift in plain red paper and tie it with a white ribbon. A handwritten message on parchment stationary, rolled into a scroll, accompanies each gift. The last evening, Christmas Eve, the giving family themselves present the final gift, the baby Jesus. The receiving family then learns who has sent their nativity set.

—*John and Trula Zimmerly, Jackson, OH*

★ To extend the fun of opening gifts we sometimes play a game. Anyone who wishes brings a small wrapped gift (unisex or gag) and places it in a large red felt stocking hanging from the mantel. "Santa" may need to have extra packages on hand, so there will be a gift for everyone. Young children receive gifts with their names on.

To play the game, designate someone to begin. (Drawing

> *"We had a friend
> make a barn for our son,
> and we added a corncrib,
> silo, and ladder
> to it."*

numbers is a good way.) The first person opens a gift. The next person may choose that gift or open a new one. Each person may choose any gift already opened, or open a new one. Anyone whose gift is taken away, immediately gets to open a new one. We set a price limit so the gifts are fairly equal in value.

—*Ellen and Paul Peachey, Harpers Ferry, WV*

★ I enjoy putting together photo albums to give as gifts. I collect pictures over the year of our son and ourselves and put them into a mini photo album as gifts for those family members whom we don't get to see much throughout the year.

—*Sara Zimmerly Ryan, Columbus, OH*

★ This Christmas, at my sister-in-law's suggestion, we did not bring wrapped gifts. Instead we were encouraged to share with each other the gift of laughter, the gift of memories, the gift of love, etc.

The sharing included a magic show by a young nephew, the reading of old and new Christmas stories, a collection of lawyer jokes from the law student in the family, a video of a musical in which a family member participated, and a slide show of old and new pictures that kindled many memories and brought forth much laughter. This has the makings of a new tradition.

—*Sarah and Herb Myers, Mount Joy, PA*

★ In earlier years, we purchased gifts for the family
throughout the year and hid them until Christmas-time. Now,
our teenage grandchildren prefer money, so they may make
their own choices and take advantage of after-Christmas
sales, making their dollars go farther. Younger grandchildren
still enjoy gifts. We aim to keep them all equal in dollar
amount.

> —*Richard and Betty Pellman, Millersville, PA*

★ When we have our family celebration (children and
grandchildren), the two older grandchildren read the names
on the gifts and the younger children are the "elves," deliver-
ing them to the proper persons. Then we take turns opening
one gift at a time while everyone watches. This means all
givers have their gifts acknowledged. We have adapted this
for the younger children by watching them open their gifts
first—not necessarily one at a time if they don't understand
the "waiting game" yet. Then the older children and adults
take turns.

> —*Earl and Margaret Sutter, Goshen, IN*

★ We spend according to the income of that year. We send
food gifts to our neighbors and friends and to widows with
children. Giving beyond our family and friends depends upon
the budget of our family that year.

> —*Thabitha, Daniel R. John Sankararto, Mary S.*
> *Rao, Mr. and Mrs. Ron Peters, Gadwal, India*

★ Our gift-giving has varied over the years. Some of the
things we've made as gifts include a child-size stove,
sink/cabinet combination, and table for our daughter. We
had a friend make a barn for our son, and we added a corn-
crib, silo, and ladder to it. I've sewn a stuffed dog and
moon/stairway shelf for two sons. Sometimes we finish
things up at 1:00 or 2:00 a.m. Christmas morning!

> —*Ernestine and Keith Lehman and family, Lititz, PA*

★ On my husband's side, we exchange names and buy gifts with a spending limit. We all contribute for a "big" gift for his parents. This year, we also gave toys to the local rescue mission.

     — *Cheryl, Lamar, Austin, and Grant Benner*
      Landisville, PA

★ We like to have small gifts available for spur-of-the-moment giving or for the children to give to teachers or friends. Hand-dipped beeswax candles have become this "small gift" tradition for our family. We use beeswax from our own beehive and make the candles ourselves. It's quite simple, and one can make a pair of beautiful 6"-7" candles in a few minutes. The smell and the feel of warm, soft, freshly dipped beeswax candles have become part of the season's magic for me.

     — *Margaret, Samuel, Bart, and Hannah*
      Wenger Johnson, Keezletown, VA

★ For many years, our family looked around during the fall to note people who were experiencing some kind of difficulty—financial, physical, or whatever. Then we tried to think how and what we could give anonymously that would lift their spirits and bring joy.

     The secrecy was a big part of the fun, but giving of ourselves was the best part, especially during those years when

things were a little short for our own family. Doing with less, so we could still give to others, was a lesson in what was really important.

—*Norman and Ruth Smith, Ailsa Craig, Ontario*

★ Some of my students whose families are from Mexico celebrate Three Kings Day (January 6) as a day for giving and receiving gifts. They place a shoe outside the door, and a parent or grandparent places small gifts or money inside. On Christmas Day they wake up early and go to their neighbors, asking for candy, and are first invited in to "Kiss the baby Jesus."

—*Elaine Shenk, Elkhart, IN*

★ One of my favorite ways to make wrapping paper is with wide-tip colorful markers on paper grocery bags. I wrap boxes with the plain side of the paper bag out, start with the name of the recipient written large, and go on to fill the paper with designs of whatever I'm inspired to make.

—*E. Elaine Kauffman, Campinas, Brazil*

★ We draw names in my extended family, as we have for about 30 years, with a $15 spending limit per gift.

Grandma goes on a shopping excursion with all of the grandchildren to the farmers market or a mall. She pays, and the gifts are spirited away to be opened at the extended family Christmas. This way she knows her gifts to them are ones they wanted.

We set up a little cardboard nativity with an array of Czech peasants and villagers, which was a gift from a Czech Brethren pastor several decades ago—it's tattered, but it glows!

—*Ruth and Timothy Stoltzfus Jost, Columbus, OH*

★ This year we made a "board" game for each family in our extended family. Also, we made favorite foods to give. We received a bird feeder, among other things.

—*Arnold and Mary K. Regier, West Liberty, OH*

> ## *"'We're inviting you to celebrate Christmas by bringing a gift for a baby.'"*

★ My husband and I often make gifts at Christmas-time. He has woodworking skills, and I enjoy sewing and painting. Sometimes we combine our skills to make gifts. Making gifts is more time-consuming than buying, but it feels more like giving from the heart! Sturdy, well-made gifts become family keepsakes.

Out of the workshop come marble rollers, wooden toys, animal train sets, and children's highback wooden chairs. Also various shelves, napkin presses, tie and belt racks, or geese pegboards. Grandchildren love to have Grandma make decorated sweat shirts, nightgowns, vests, fabric clutch purses. Adults like my doorstop dolls, aprons, and casserole carriers. Craft magazines give me ideas.

—Esther and Dave Kniss, Gulfport, MS

★ One year our extended family decided to give gifts to the local pregnancy center instead of having our usual grab-bag gift exchange. The notice that went to the family members read as follows: "Christmas is the celebration of a birth, a baby's birth. That baby appeared to be illegitimate, poor, perhaps even homeless. That baby was Jesus, who grew to be the Christ, the savior of the world! This year, instead of a grab-bag, we're inviting you to celebrate Christmas by bringing a gift for a baby. The baby may be illegitimate, poor, or even homeless. It will be a baby born to someone who is being ministered to by the local pregnancy center. We hope the baby will grow to be a Christian, someone who will share the good news of Christ, the savior of the world. Bring the gifts to the family gathering unwrapped so everyone can see them. Spend as much, or as little, as you like. Gifts may be new, or as-good-as-new."

> —*Mary Lahman*
> *Heatwole*
> *Harrisonburg, VA*

★ We grandparents send checks at Thanksgiving time to our children to buy gifts for themselves and the grandchildren. They bring the grandchildren's gifts along to be opened at the extended family Christmas gift exchange. (This seems like a cop-out, but we are not up on contemporary children's books and games!)

> —*Chester and Sara*
> *Jane Wenger, Lancaster PA*

★ In the last few years, we have asked each of our five children to write a letter, telling about their year's activities and some of the thoughts and experiences they have had. These have come to be a greater "gift" than all the material things used to be.

> —*John L. and Beulah E. Fretz, Salem, OR*

★ My husband has made over 200 yule logs to give to Sunday school teachers, school teachers, newcomers to the church, new neighbors, and special friends. He gets a log, drills holes for two or three red candles, adds a Christmas decoration, pine cones, and ribbon. The children help, as they are able, to trim the log. As a family we take the log to the home of the recipient with the candles burning and give the recipient a "Merry Christmas."

> —*Joyce Eigsti Hofer, Denver, CO*

★ We often buy a turkey for a poor family, as well as for our own family, encouraging our children to give some of their allowance to help to pay for the gift turkey.

—Beth Weaver Bonnar Nelson, British Columbia

★ Christmas is one time we "pull out all the stops" to celebrate the most important birthday ever. Yet we don't spend a lot on material gifts. We make things by hand, participate in programs, and distribute food boxes from the food bank. We concentrate on quality family times and inviting other to share a good meal.

—David and Louisa Mow, Farmington, PA

★ This year, instead of wrapping paper, we used brown paper bags which the children decorated by dipping cookie cutters into paint and putting imprints on the bags. When the bags were filled with a gift, we folded the tops down once, punched two holes in the center a few inches apart, and tied a ribbon through to fasten them. We also used cartoons from Sunday newspapers as a colorful, cheap wrapping paper.

—John and Sandra Drescher-Lehman, Richmond, VA

★ When my husband and I make wooden gifts for the children (such as trains, barns, marble rollers, etc.), we often don't have them finished by Christmas Day. The whole family works together on completing the gifts and enjoys them just as much in January or February as they would have were the gifts actually finished on Christmas Day!

—Helen Stoltzfus Bowman, Millersburg, IN

★ When our grandchildren turn 13, we give them a good quality Bible. (My grandparents did this when we became members of the church. That was usually around our 13th birthdays.)

Erma Kauffman, Cochranville, PA

★ This year we gave the extended family a genealogy that we did of our family—we included pictures we discovered and reproduced for everyone.

— *Mrs. Donald Roggie, Lowville, NY*

★ We usually know a needy family through our apartment business, for whom we buy gifts. Perhaps we get a turkey and some money for food; then, as a family, we take these gifts to them. It helps our kids to look beyond, "What am I getting for Christmas?" to, "How can I help someone else have Christmas?" (We do buy gifts for each other, too.)

— *Judy Stoltzfus, Colorado Springs, CO*

★ After we sold our big house and moved into an apartment, we could no longer entertain four children and their spouses, 10 grandchildren, and two great-grandchildren. One year our Christmas gift to the children was an expense-free stay at a motel. It was such a satisfying experience that we repeated it two years later. By then, each family paid their way.

We request no gifts for ourselves. What do you get people who have everything they need? (A little cheating in gift-giving goes on anyway, in good fun.) The grandchildren draw names among themselves.

— *Frank and Marie Wiens, Hillsboro, KS*

★ One year before we left college for the Christmas holiday, we were challenged to do some unexpected thing for someone in our home community. I baked some wonderful rings and iced raised sweet breads and took the delicacies to some elderly neighbors back home. This started a tradition of baking for the neighbors which I have continued to this day. I include all the neighbors whose land adjoins ours. This year I went with a card and a wrapped loaf of banana bread, and had a delightful visit with each family.

A yearly contact keeps me in touch with all of these people, and adds to my personal assurance. I know that my neighbors, whom I seldom see, are my friends, and they know that I am here and am available if a need arises.

— Mary Jane Lederach Hershey, Harleysville, PA

★ I got a homemade tablecloth from my son-in-law this year!

— Jewel Showalter, Landisville, PA

★ We don't like drawing names for immediate family (children, grandchildren). We try to determine special needs, with no set spending limit, but go with what common sense and stewardship dictate.

— Mrs. Lou Maniaci, Gladstone, MI

★ One Christmas I made housecoats or robes for the grandchildren. I made a flannel robe for our three-year-old grandson—it came the whole way to the floor. Several years later he came to spend the night with us, and wore the flannel robe when he was ready for bed. His mother said it was his constant companion. Now it came up to his knees, and was just about too tight!

— Mary E. Martin, Goshen, IN

★ My extended family's gift exchange has included some unique homemade gifts. Some of the ideas—a tent pole bag (made of corduroy appliqued with a camping scene, bringing back memories of our annual Moyer family camporee), a flannel nightgown, a folding camp table, a handmade food dehydrator, and fresh cinnamon buns.

A yearly gift for our family has always been a new children's Christmas book. Each year we get out the whole pile early in December and read, read, read.

— *Elaine and Jim Gibbel, Lititz, PA*

> *"This started a tradition*
> *of baking for the neighbors*
> *which I have continued*
> *to this day.*
> *I include all the neighbors*
> *whose land adjoins ours."*

★ Rather than buy gifts for our grandchildren, I make wooden toys for the boys until they are six years old. When they are six years old, I buy them a tool box. Each year when they are between six and 16, I buy them a tool. After they turn 16 they receive cash. Edith makes items for the girls—bunnies, dolls, clothing. At age 16, the grandchildren all receive an "antique car," a wooden one that I've made!

— *David and Edith Thomas, Lancaster, PA*

★ We try to imagine the perfect gift—and one year my husband hit the bull's eye. I had to carry a very heavy fax machine home with me for weekends "on call," and that year his gift to me was a petite but strong luggage carrier.

This year our daughter's gift to her 22-year-old brother was four tickets to an ice hockey game—we all went.

— *Marj and Delbert Wiens, Fresno, CA*

> *"One year I bought a picture album*
> *for each of our children*
> *and partly filled each one*
> *with old memory pictures."*

★ My brother-in-law and his wife regularly give to relief organizations, in *our* name during the holidays. This year they/we gave Habitat for Humanity three pieces of drywall and two pounds of nails. I appreciated that gift more than having something delivered to my doorstep by UPS.

One of my husband's brothers and his wife have taken it upon themselves to be responsible for a family calendar that we all receive as a Christmas gift. They make use of a national photo company for printing, but do spend many hours themselves sorting through family photos. Pictures of the four brothers as children and college students, of Mom and Dad, and now of wives and grandchildren bring back great memories and spark lots of laughter from family and friends. This year's theme was "Then and Now" with pictures of the boys as children/young adults, and then of them with their families. Other themes could be vacation highlights, Christmases past and present, etc. We'd like to add birthdays and anniversaries printed on the appropriate days.

— *Connie Faber, Hillsboro, KS*

★ We always encouraged our children to write thank-you notes to the senders of their gifts.

— *Faye and Harry Pankratz, Inola, OR*

★ Gift-giving has been very important to us, but never all-consuming. We always tried to put three gifts for each child under the tree—one to read, one to wear, and one gift which they could enjoy or use in many ways.

— *Norma J. Pauls, Oakville, Ontario*

★ Since many of my friends are getting married, having families, and/or buying homes, we all have less money for gift-giving. We have chosen to do "something special" together over the holidays, rather than giving gifts. As our lives become busier, the gift of time together is more and more special.

—Dawn J. Ranck, Strasburg, PA

★ I know one family who draws names and sets an arbitrary amount ($4.37, for example) which has to be spent on the gift. They have a wonderful time going to thrift stores and garage sales to see what they can come up with.

We've started a tradition of giving coupons to each other. This requires more creativity, as well as sacrificial giving on the part of each person. It also can be done by the very young, up to and including those who are adults. Coupons can include anything: an evening out with Daddy (one-on-one), a song, a backrub, an evening of milkshakes, free babysitting, or a hug.

We try to stress to our children that gifts are given at Christmas because the wise men gave gifts to Jesus. The way we can give gifts to Jesus is explained in the Bible. "Whatever you did for one of the least of these who are members of my family, you did for me." (Matthew 25:40)

—Kay Driver, Columbus, OH

★ We like to make our gifts whenever we can. We have made coffee tables, magazine racks, wooden nativity puzzle sets, napkin holders, lamps, and wooden trains—using some 14 different kinds of wood.

One year I bought a picture album for each of our children and partly filled each one with old memory pictures. This gift did not cost much, but took a lot of time and love to prepare. (Our children and grandchildren exchange names.)

The last few years, sometime during December, we invite several families for dinner whom we have become acquainted with through our quadriplegic son. Members of these families work with him, doing his personal care. We have small gift exchanges with them, also.

—*Marjora Miller, Archbold, OH*

★ I mail little gifts because it's fun to get surprises in the mail.

—*Jane Brubaker, Leaburg, OR*

★ This year for our gift exchange within the extended family, we chose paper as a theme and set a price limit of $7. Peter thinned his library by giving away books. To his eldest sister he gave "How to Enjoy Aging"; to another (single) sister who often askes him financial advice, a book on "Financial Investments"; to another almost-or-near retiring couple, "How to Retire and Enjoy It." In all, he gave away 17 books. Now he can buy more!

—*Peter and Susan Kehler, Sumas, WA*

★ We have adapted to our changing family by starting a Sisters Christmas Tradition. Our parents are elderly; the grandkids all grown. So we three sisters who live within reasonable driving distance go out to eat and exchange small gifts sometime during the Christmas season. (Our brother is excluded—because he lives out of state!) This is a siblings-only get-together (no spouses).

— *Grace Nolt, Canadensis, PA*

★ We've started a tradition of making Christmas candles for other children—the same age, size, sex of our children—as a concrete way of giving to needy children.

— *Carol and Jim Spicher, Mountville, PA*

6.

Ideas for Making Shopping Bearable and Even Meaningful

> *"They shut the door,*
> *and, after scurrying around,*
> *they came pushing a box,*
> *saying,*
> *'We want to give*
> *you something, too!'"*

★ One of my best friends and I usually do a December shopping day for Christmas. This is the only time of year we get together in this way because we are not big on shopping. It is always a fun day, and we get a lot accomplished.

—*Mary Lois and Lloyd Kreider, Oxford, PA*

★ The first time our children thought about giving as well as receiving was when our son was only four years old, and our daughter three. After opening their gifts, our son suddenly dropped his gift and whispered to his sister to come into the hall. They shut the door, and, after scurrying around, they came pushing a box, saying, "We want to give you something, too!"

Never mind that it was filled with some of the clothes from the laundry that hadn't been put into the drawers yet! It truly was the thought behind the gift that brought tears to our eyes. When they were a little older, we gave them each an amount of money. They pooled that money to buy each sibling one gift and one for us as parents. Even when they pooled their money instead of each buying for each, the gifts weren't really big, but the love wasn't skimpy!

—*Norman and Ruth Smith, Ailsa Craig, Ontario*

★ We've made a tradition of going shopping the day after Thanksgiving, although we start looking for gifts as early as May.

—*Keith and Gail Pentz, Casselberry, FL*

★ We do not want to join the rush. We carefully make (highly selective) lists, just to buy *useful* things. We always utilize good opportunities (not necessarily during Christmas), but three or four times per year whenever there are grand-sales, as our budget allows. We do it all together.
— *Charles and Lisa Christano, Kiedus, Indonesia*

★ I think, brainstorm, and form a specific list in advance of shopping. I try to plan (as much as possible) my shopping route. This past year I did most of my shopping in one evening. It helps, too, to write down gift ideas throughout the year.
— *Melanie Gochnauer, Columbia, PA*

★ A friend of mine knows a man who shopped for a Christmas present for his wife and always took their three boys along. Every year they went to a department store and picked out a lovely nightgown. They had it gift-wrapped and then went out for lunch. This made a particularly big impression on the boys as they became teenagers.
— *Joyce Eigsti Hofer, Denver, CO*

★ One year we decided to buy early at my sister's store in Texas—but burglars later broke into our house and stole all our gifts!
— *Faye and Harry Pankratz, Inola, OR*

★ A number of years ago, my husband took a vacation day from work and we began an annual trip to a nearby town to the different malls, starting with breakfast and making a big day of it. This has become a tradition for us which we really enjoy.
— *Ernestine and Keith Lehman and family, Lititz, PA*

★ I make most of the gifts, starting in January.
— *Debra Bachman, Pomeroy, IA*

★ When I was growing up, my family often delayed opening gifts until a few days after Christmas. This allowed everyone to take advantage of after-Christmas sales when buying gifts for each other. Often we went out one day as a family to shop, splitting up for a few hours when we reached the designated shopping location.

By waiting for all this until after Christmas, we had more of a focus on family, extended family, and being thankful for Christ's birth on Christmas day itself.
— *Suzanne Marie Hitt, Fairfield, OH*

★ My mom shops early in the year as she finds things. I tend to wait for inspiration, and then get caught in last minute frenzied shopping malls. I like to shop at Self-Help

stores for gifts because their items are unique and beautiful and they feel like an alternative to the local mall.
— *Elaine Shenk, Elkhart, IN*

★ My husband always takes a day off from work in mid-December, and we go shopping together. We always eat lunch out somewhere. I look forward to that day.
— *Cindy Horning, Denver, PA*

★ Grandma usually checks with the parents regarding appropriate gifts for the grandchildren, then shops accordingly and hopes not to cause any undue disappointments. Grandpa is in charge of giving the monetary gifts to the adults.

Every year Grandma makes some special small gifts for her granddaughters, such as potholders, vests, or embroidered hand towels.

Everyone, adults and grandchildren, always gets to pick a red delicious apple and a large orange. During the family gathering, bowls of popcorn and peanuts and dishes of Christmas candies are available for all.
— *Wilmer A. and Esther M. Harms*
   North Newton, KS

★ I often catalog-shop since I'm not particularly fond of shopping. All four of us (our kids are 18 and 21) shop for one another. We scout garage sales and specialty shops for that "special gag" gift we can hardly wait to give to the unsuspecting person. We usually give these gifts on Christmas Eve.
— *Barb Hershey, Lancaster, PA*

★ This year I did very little shopping—I distributed family mementoes among my three daughters and their families. Some of the treasures came from great- and great-great-grandparents. I also had old photos remade. They were appreciated, too.
— *Norma Pletscher True, Santa Fe, NM*

★ I try to shop all year long. I have found some wonderful gifts after Christmas that I save for the next year. I also keep an ongoing list of things I buy throughout the year so I remember what I have purchased.

> *— Clark, Cindy, Lara, and Hilary Breeze*
> *Champaign, IL*

★ One year we found a good peace book and gave one copy to each family of cousins.

> *— Rod and Martha Yoder Maust, Indianapolis, IN*

★ We make gifts early, like chutney of extra green tomatoes, and we gather natural "leavings" to make swags and wallhangings. We make lists, let them sit, and then review them again before settling on definite gifts. Then we are able to do shopping either by mail or in one or two trips to town.

> *— Kirsten Zerger, McPherson, KS*

★ Our present pattern involves very little shopping. I am so glad for that, because I have never enjoyed shopping at any season, and I find Christmas an especially sad time to be in stores. Everyone seems hurried; it all seems so artificial and wrong, somehow. I do what little I need to as early as possible, and then stay away from malls and stores—especially malls!

> *— Mary Ellen and Albert Meyer, Goshen, IN*

> *"I find Christmas*
> *an especially sad time*
> *to be in stores.*
> *Everyone seems hurried;*
> *it all seems so*
> *artificial and wrong, somehow."*

> *"We would buy
> the gifts together
> without a lot of looking,
> which pleased him,
> and I had the satisfaction
> of receiving his opinion and advice,
> which pleased me."*

★ Usually we make one or two shopping days or excursions a few weeks before Christmas to our local shopping centers. It becomes a time of togetherness for the two of us.

— *Fred and Margaret Heese, Wymark, Saskatchewan*

★ Before we go shopping, each of us decides about how much money we will spend on each person. Then we each write up a "wish list" which we show to the rest of the family. From these lists, we choose which gifts to buy before we go shopping. This method saves lots of time and headaches. We also try to make some homemade gifts.

— *Mary, Wayne, Alison, and Megan Nitzsche*
Wooster, OH

★ I have begun ordering a one-year magazine subscription for each grandchild. This takes some time and careful discrimination, but less walking in malls and shops.

Shopping time is shorter and gift enjoyment longer.

— *Walter and Lorene Good, Armington, IL*

★ I like to "shop" by picking up the telephone and ordering from catalogs. That is much easier than walking the malls. I start early and usually am finished by early December.

— *Sarah Yoder Scott, Newark, DE*

★ We shop secretly for our immediate family. We usually try to include some gifts of humor and/or practical application. These gifts may be homemade, or be bought for $5 or less. We then give the gifts by drawing lots. From that moment on, we barter, trade, and even engage in outright "forced" exchange! It's a way to have fun and also a way to learn from each other.

— *Clare and Ben Neufeld, Delta, British Columbia*

★ When we were married, my husband declared, "I don't like to shop!"

I felt I really needed his help in making decisions, so we worked things out this way: on a Sunday afternoon or weekday evening, we would sit down together and make a list of the people we planned to buy for, coming up with one or two gift suggestions for each one. Then I would shop, eliminating the places where it was no use to look, and choosing the places where I could find the best buys.

After that, my husband would take one day and shopping with me. We bought the gifts together without a lot of looking, which pleased him, and I had the satisfaction of receiving his opinion and advice, which pleased me. We had dinner together in a nice restaurant on shopping day, and that pleased both of us.

Resistance to Christmas shopping gradually decreased, and one year my husband admitted that he enjoyed the day! My joy was complete the year *he asked me,* "When are we going Christmas shopping?"

—*Mary Lahman Heatwole, Harrisonburg, VA*

7.

Christmas Eve: Ideas and Traditions

Note: There are many ideas for Christmas Eve in earlier chapters. Here are additional ones.

★ We have a tradition of filling stockings for each other on Christmas Eve. Parents did it just for children until they were old enough to provide stockings for parents. Now, everyone sneaks in sometime on Christmas Eve and slips little surprises into the stockings.

We usually have lasagna on Christmas Eve. One recipe is vegetarian and one is not.
— *Joyce G. Zuercher, Hesston, KS*

★ We open one gift at a time to assure that each gift is fully appreciated for itself and is not lost in an orgy of paper-ripping and loot-gathering. This takes longer, but ultimately makes the process feel better and brings us all together in sharing-the-bounty-of-the-season.
— *Kirsten Zerger, McPherson, KS*

★ Since we've lived in Elkhart, our Christmas Eve celebration includes a stop for hot drinks at the home of good friends. Then we drive to Notre Dame to the Christmas Eve Midnight Mass. Christmas hasn't really come until we step out of the church about 1:30 a.m. into the cold crisp air and walk across the campus, hearing the church bells ringing wildly.
— *Marlene and Stanley Kropf, Elkhart, IN*

★ We work with native American Indian communities here in the Chaco of Argentina. Christmas and New Year's are big celebrations for them. This year there was an open air church service from 8 p.m. to midnight, followed by stew, homemade bread, and watermelon. There are also lots of fireworks for Christmas and New Year's.
— *Becky Wigginton, Chaco, Argentina*

★ When the children were small, they liked to go on treasure hunts to find their gifts. After about two or three clues, the fourth clue would read something like this—"Have hot chocolate and cookies together as a family before you get your next clue." Now that the children are teenagers, we play the game Rook. When a person wins a hand, he or she gets to open a gift.
— *Dennis, Sharon, Daniel, and Heather Showalter*
West Liberty, Ohio

> *"I learned that caroling
> wasn't only fun and games—
> it meant muddy roads,
> cold feet,
> and tired voices."*

★ Typically, Jordanian Christians put up a Christmas tree shortly before Christmas, all churches have a Christmas morning worship service, regardless of the day of week, and Christmas day is spent with one's nuclear family or the closest of extended family. The next couple days are spent in many short visits to relatives, neighbors, and friends. At each visit you are served coffee, homemade or bought cookies, and sometimes tea. Upon leaving you are always served from an attractive plate of chocolates and other candies. These holiday visits can go on for several weeks, although it is most intensive the first couple of days.

Jordan is a Muslim country, so Christmas is not a national holiday. However, the Christian minority is by law allowed to take off work and school for Christmas and the following day.

In addition to chocolates for visitors, special cookies and bread are made for the holidays. The cookies, called *Ka'ak*, are yeast dough made from flour or cream of wheat and stuffed with date or nut fillings. *Gras* (pronounced like the beginning of *gracias*) is a thick pita bread made with turmeric (to make it yellow) and other special seasonings. Each loaf is pressed into a carved wooden mold before baking to imprint pretty designs.

Except for the baking, little happens before Christmas. The "holiday season" is Christmas Day and the following days. Gifts are mainly for children and are often clothes.

—Jeanne Shirk Sahawneh, Irbid, Jordan

★ I grew up in a rural church with a longstanding tradition of all the young people going Christmas Eve caroling to all the families of the congregation. Our family would rush home from the children's Christmas Eve program, open our gifts from one another, enjoy a hot drink and some cookies, and prepare for caroling.

We formed two groups, split the church family list, and eagerly started on our night's project. Most of the members of our congregation resided in the country, which meant lots of driving. The sponsors and upperclassmen were experts at locating the right bedroom windows and knowing which homes provided snacks, regardless of the hour.

I learned that caroling wasn't only fun and games—it meant muddy roads, cold feet, and tired voices. We'd plan a warm-up stop midway, and finally would conclude about 4 a.m. at someone's home. The parents in that "lucky" home would prepare a nourishing meal. We seemed to find enough energy to eagerly down the food, and then collapse in tired heaps on the floor for a few minutes before heading home for a few hours of sleep.

—*Connie Faber, Hillsboro, KS*

★ With our grown family, we have caroled for friends, taking pecan pies as gifts. Several years I baked up to 10 pecan pies as gifts. We delivered them, singing. Lots of fun! In the snow, too.

— Gladys and Merv Rutt, Blue Ball, PA

★ We take pictures so we can remember what presents we received each year.

— Judy Stoltzfus, Colorado Springs, CO

★ The most special things about our late dinners is that we always set one extra place—for the Christ child, the family of strangers who couldn't join us or, in the past four years, to represent our deceased daughter.

— Winifred Ewy, Newton, KS

★ Every other year, Christmas Eve is extra special at Grandpa and Grandma's house because everyone in the family sleeps over. We set up cots, bring in sleeping bags, and the house brims with people and activity. After a soup supper, we may laugh with old slides, share an old tape or record, and sometimes have our gift exchange. The Christmas story is read, recited, or acted out by the children. Young pianists may "try out" on some Christmas carols, while adults try to keep in time with the music.

— Lois and J. Lester Brubaker, Smoketown, PA

> *"It's a quiet, festive time,*
> *until someone drops their bread*
> *into the fondue*
> *and needs to kiss the person on their right."*

★ While some of us are busy with supper preparations, the rest are putting together special Christmas treats for our 100 chickens, our cats, and dogs. We give the chickens extra feed or hot mash, and this year our cats, and dogs got their own platter of fried hamburger!

After all the preparations, we have a quiet yet festive time as we sit down together to a candle-lit cheese fondue. (Quiet that is, until someone drops their bread into the fondue and needs to kiss the person on their right!)
— *Helen Stoltzfus Bowman, Millersburg, IN*

★ Here the big moment is midnight on Christmas Eve when it is traditional to have supper. Children take extra naps in the afternoon so they can stay awake, but some simply fall asleep, and that's just fine, too.

Friends who are far from their families, as I am, and some whose families do not celebrate, like to get together for this Christmas Eve supper. We plan in advance who will bring what.
— *E. Elaine Kauffman, Campinas, SP, Brazil*

★ We light candles, watch some movies, and feast on homemade soup and cookies. We open *one* gift.
— *Jane Brubaker, Leaburg, OR*

★ One year my siblings and parents were in four different countries at Christmas. We figured out the time change and designated one hour to think of and pray for each other on Christmas night. We were together in spirit, though far apart.
— *Karen Miller Rush, Harrisonburg, VA*

★ One year we came home from the Christmas Eve service at church and frosted our cookies. It was such fun that it became a tradition. The children invited their friends for cookie decorating, or we would invite an elderly person or two to come home from church with us to join the party, share their creativity, and take some cookies home.

—James and Anna Juhnke, North Newton, KS

★ We invite single neighbors to drop in during the evening for food and conversation.

—Dawn Pichette, Harbor City, CA

★ On Christmas Eve, we light all the many candles in the house and turn off or dim all the electric lights. The children get to do the candlelighting at dusk, and fragrant candles make the house smell wonderful.

—Ned and Debbi Wyse, Camden, MI

★ Christmas Eve for our family is probably the best part of Christmas. It has the feeling that "everything is ready" and it is full of anticipation for the next day. We always have a wonderful early dinner of two kinds of soup. Then we play a grab-bag gift game that we started over 15 years ago.

After dinner and the gift game, we always go to our church service. Following that we have a time of fellowship in the church basement.

Our family then piles into the car and goes to several of the well-known spots in the area which have huge Christmas light displays. After getting home, the kids go to bed, and we fill the stockings. Everyone gets a stocking in our house.

—Clark, Cindy, Lara, and Hilary Breeze
Champaign, IL

★ Several times we have slept in front of the fireplace in sleeping bags.

—Erma Wenger, Lancaster, PA

> *"We never miss hearing
> the real heartbeat of each person
> during our otherwise
> rather raucous get-togethers."*

★ We have our (nuclear) family Christmas on Christmas Eve. We schedule the extended family Christmas for any date we can make.

The treasured custom has been "circle time" when adults meet and each takes five to 10 minutes to say what has been most important in the past year. It takes several hours. In this way, in our family of extroverts, we never miss hearing the real heartbeat of each person during our otherwise rather raucous get-togethers.

—*Ruth and Timothy Stoltzfus Jost
Columbus, OH*

★ In our family, since the children are no longer living at home, they come home Christmas Eve for supper and to spend the night. Grand-children open their stocking stuffers after supper. Every other year, when children and grand-children go to the "other grandparents," we pick another night as our family's "Christmas Eve."

A traditional main dish for several years for Christmas Eve supper has been Taco Twist Casserole, with go-alongs.

—*Richard and Betty
Pellman
Millersville, PA*

★ We go to Catholic mass (even though we aren't Catholic). It is a special night and a special way to remember Jesus being born. I especially like the candles, the huge group of people there, the loud organ, and the high ceiling with ornate decorations.

—*Sara Zimmerly Ryan, Columbus, OH*

★ We have celebrated Christmas Eve in the German tradition for as long as I can remember. Everyone goes to Oma's (my mother's) house after the church service. Here we sit around the Christmas tree, do some singing, and the children say their memorized poems or sing a special song they learned in school or Sunday school.

Not soon enough for the little ones, one or two of them are asked to be *Weihnachtsman* and hand out the gifts to be opened. We enjoy nuts, oranges, and candies. Each family gets a bag of Oma's special Christmas honey and star anise cookies, as well as an envelope with card and money. Oma and the great-grandchildren open gifts, and then we all enjoy more fruit and ham or meatballs. Children can stay up late,

even though they will be up early to see what is under the tree at home on Christmas morning, and then be in church for the service at 10 a.m.

—Jake and Herta Janzen, Coledale, Alberta

★ We are usually at home on Christmas Eve. It is a quiet reflective time, filled with music and lake-watching.

—Florence Duley and Merlin Wideman
Sherwood Park, Alberta

★ The crowning of the season is Christmas Eve, when church members and young people stage a live nativity outdoors, complete with animals and a real baby. We sing and read the Christmas story from the gospel. All go home, then, to their Christmas Eve dinner with candles they have lit at the manger, symbolic of the light we receive from Christ.

—David and Louisa Mow, Farmington, PA

★ After a family gets together, they each go out to look for their friends whom they do not see regularly during the year. Children seek their peers, and young people do the same, as well as the adults. They spend the whole night together until the 4:00 a.m. church service. Since our houses are so close to each other, no one needs a chaperon. Food is everywhere. Even if you don't know the family, you can just go and eat. It is an honor for them to have you as a guest.

—Luis A. Lumibao, San Jose City, Philippines

★ Every year we invite friends and neighbors to celebrate Christmas Eve in our home. Generally we have 45-55 people. Children and adults of all ages come. We have a short program with a lot of carol-singing. After the program, everyone enjoys hot apple cider, coffee, tea, punch, and a variety of homemade Christmas baking which is brought by each of the families as they arrive. The program begins at 6:30 so it is over early enough for everyone to get home in good time.

—Norma J. Pauls, Oakville, Ontario

★ We gather around Grandma's organ, and she accompanies us as we sing carols.
> —*Heidi Eash, Bristol, IN*

★ Christmas Eve always means attending the early Christmas Eve candlelight service at our church. On the way home we usually drive around the town to see the Christmas lights and luminaries, stopping by the Moravian church to hear the Trombone Choir in the church square. At home we enjoy Christmas music, cookies, and eggnog in the living room, admiring our tree.
> —*Jim and Elaine Gibbel, Lititz, PA*

★ On Christmas Eve we always watch home movies of when we four girls were younger. Then we go to church for the midnight service. After that we go to the waffle house around 1:00 a.m. for coffee.
> —*Abbie Berkshire, Harrisonburg, VA*

★ Almost every Christmas we read *The Best Christmas Pageant Ever* as a family.
> —*Melodie Horst, Harrisonburg, VA*

★ After our candlelight Christmas Eve service at church, we join three other families with whom we have shared many experiences, beginning with high school. We bring finger food to share. Our adult children, who are no longer living at home, look forward to this time to reconnect with friends they grew up with.
> —*Herb and Sarah Myers, Mount Joy, PA*

★ My in-laws collect every candle in the house, and we have oyster stew by candlelight after church.
> —*Joe and Laura Bare, New Braunfels, TX*

8.
Christmas Day: Ideas and Traditions

Note: There are many dozens of ideas for Christmas Day in earlier chapters. Here are additional ones.

★ I know families who designate a room in the house as "The Christmas Room." This room is shrouded in mystery and is kept locked from all but the parents. On Christmas morning at the sound of a bell, all may enter the decorated room and enjoy the gifts laid out under one or more Christmas trees.

One year we set up an intercom so we could hear our children's early morning discoveries of their stockings from our bed. We also made a tape of it and sent it to Grandma. It was delightful.

—David and Louisa Mow, Farmington, PA

★ This past Christmas we made graham cracker houses as a family. Everyone participated—it was a wonderful way to spend the day—a tradition we'll probably continue. The houses ranged from a house with an outhouse guarded by a gummy alligator, to a house with a fallen telephone pole, which later had a vehicle crash added to it!

—Dawn J. Ranck, Strasburg, PA

★ For years we began a large jigsaw puzzle over the holidays as part of our entertainment. However, a kitten in our home changed that tradition. It, too, liked puzzles, but didn't follow the rules!

—Michael, Lena, Lowell, and Miriam Brown, Grantham, PA

★ Our family has always invited another family for Christmas dinner. They are generally, if not always, a family far away from home, with no family close by with whom they can celebrate Christmas. Often we ask the guest family to bring one of their own traditional dishes to the dinner to make it more like their own familiar Christmas. We try to have families with young children, if possible.

—Norma J. Pauls, Oakville, Ontario

★ We wrapped small gifts for each person, using lots of tape. Then we passed the gifts around and around, until the music stopped. When the music stopped, each person started tearing the wrappings off the package she or he was holding. When the music started again, everyone had to pass on the gift each had held. When a gift was unwrapped, the person who finished it kept the gift. (Only one gift per person.) We kept going until all of the gifts were opened.
—*Marjora Miller, Archbold, OH*

★ Christmas morning begins with opening stocking gifts, a favorite Christmas tradition with our daughters which began years ago when they were small. Christmas then usually meant taking long car trips to grandparents. To help pass the time while we drove, we took their filled stockings along. Based on the length of the trip and the number of gifts in the stockings, they opened gifts at set time intervals. The trip went fast and the girls were happy, occupied with their unwrapped treasures.
—*Herb and Sarah Myers, Mount Joy, PA*

★ We always have oyster stew and chili on Christmas Eve— and put the leftover oysters and milk into the dressing for Christmas Day. Now that we've started to raise chestnuts, we're including them in the dressing—getting back to earlier traditions when chestnuts were plentiful.

We always play games—and there's always one large new jigsaw puzzle which provides a group activity, camaraderie, and an intergenerational "fun" focus.

—*John and Betty Wittrig, Winfield, IA*

★ When I was a child, we always went to the city a few days before Christmas to be with my grandparents. My aunt was farsighted and realized that Christmas Day took forever to come in the eyes of children. She always let each of us open one special gift the night before the big gift opening. I still remember the locket I got when I was 12 years old.

—*Joyce Eigsti Hofer, Denver, CO*

★ Many years we've made a tape recording at various times throughout the day. It is interesting to listen to them years later, recalling some of those wonderful occasions.

—*Keith and Ernestine Lehman and family*
Lititz, PA

★ In the Indian communities, there is usually a morning church service, followed by baptism. This year the temperature was very hot.

—*Becky Wigginton, Chaco, Argentina*

*"I still remember
the locket I got
when I was 12 years old."*

★ On Christmas morning we still have the routine of chores on the dairy farm, and then a short church service. If we have overnight guests, or know of a needy person nearby, they share our hearty breakfast. If there is snow, everybody goes tobogganing behind the tractor or three-wheeler.
— *Hilda J. Born, Abbotsford, British Columbia*

★ Christmas morning breakfast is the most special tradition of the whole year at Grandpa and Grandma Brubaker's house. The table centerpiece provides an aroma of burning candles and evergreens from the backyard. Fresh fruit plates, a tea ring with Jesus' birthday candle, and a round wooden crown with candles for each member of the family adorn the red tablecloth. We begin with the candle-lighting ceremony and litany of thanks for family.

We grandparents light our center candles, and then, as each of our children and their spouses light their candles, we bless them by saying, "You, our children, are a gift of God to us." Each of our children similarly blesses their children as they light their candles.

The fully lighted crown is glowing as we join in saying, "We are all special to each other because of Jesus' love in us." After Grandma leads in prayer, we light the Jesus candle and sing "Happy Birthday" to Jesus. We then enjoy our breakfast and rejoice in the blessing of being together.
— *Lois and J. Lester Brubaker, Smoketown, PA*

★ Many times my husband and I have been alone on Christmas Day. So we've gone to a nearby city, taken a nature walk, seen a movie. Sometimes we have pizza and

Pepsi in Christmas goblets. Christmas dinner (turkey, natural-ly) is for when our sons and their families can be with us.

— *Esther Bixler Heatwole, Rocky Ford, CO*

★ We try to keep Christmas Day quiet, reflective, and fami-ly-oriented. The children find their stockings filled, so we open these together. By separating gifts from stockings (gifts on Christmas Eve and stockings on Christmas Day), we spread out the fun and lessen the overwhelming sense of riches, which is so hard for the children to handle, and which causes such blues when it's over.

Stockings contain small gifts which are often more fun than the bigger items from the night before. The day pro-ceeds at a slow pace—a good, special meal, naps, walks outdoors, family games. Basically we try to create a Sabbath Day to receive and recognize the special spirit which Christmas is meant to honor.

— *Kirsten Zerger, McPherson, KS*

> *"We were not allowed to go downstairs*
> *until we heard Grandma*
> *playing 'Silent Night' on the piano."*

★ We usually set the table with an orange that had its skin cut down from the top in wedges almost to the bottom, then folded down toward the orange and the ends tucked in underneath. The sections were separated, again almost to the bottom, and a red grape or plum date pushed down in the middle to create a flower effect. The rest of the menu changed from time to time, but everyone counts on that orange being there.

— *Norman and Ruth Smith, Ailsa Craig, Ontario*

★ During my childhood, we always spent the Christmas holidays at my grandparents' home; my cousins and aunts and uncle from Colorado went there, too. On Christmas morning, we were not allowed to go downstairs until we heard Grandma playing "Silent Night" on the piano. Then we all joined her in singing it as we came downstairs. Once we saw our stockings, though, the song was forgotten in the excitement! Later, after breakfast, we opened our presents under the Christmas tree.

After Larry and I married and the children came, we developed a similar tradition. On Christmas morning, no one goes to the living room alone. When everyone is up, we go together, cameras in hand to snap the excitement. A stockingful of new things, even small things, carries each child through breakfast. After breakfast we gather around our Christmas tree and read the Christmas story from Luke. When the girls were young, they enjoyed acting it out as we read it. (A Cabbage Patch baby doll was baby Jesus for several years.) For our gift exchange, we take turns handing out one or two gifts to each person. After we open those and admire each other's, it is time to hand out some more.

—*Janet, Larry, Susan, and Kara Dixon, Topeka, KS*

★ We sleep in on Christmas morning! After all that late food—what else?
—*E. Elaine Kauffman, Campinas, SP, Brazil*

★ Mother spent most of the morning wrestling with the goose and the rest of the meal. Dad helped the little ones with their new toys. After the traditional dinner, unless it was raining, we all bundled up and went for a long walk. Quite often we drove the 10 miles to the state park and walked 3½ miles around Lake Argyle. Back home again, we played games until it was time to go to bed.
—*Grace and Werner Will, Stevensville, MT*

★ This year, for the first time, we rented a camp in North Carolina to celebrate Christmas.
—*Miriam Shoup, Orrville, OH*

★ To alleviate a "let-down" feeling on December 26, we usually gave our children a new puzzle or game that day which they could enjoy together.
—*Ellen and Paul Peachey, Harpers Ferry, WV*

★ Christmas Day is a day to wait for people to come and visit, especially people from other provinces.
—*Luis A. Lumibao, San Jose City, Philippines*

★ Christmas morning begins with a festive breakfast: fresh baked cinnamon rolls (from Mother's recipe), a variety of fruits, apple sausage, a baked egg and cheese casserole, and plenty of good coffee. Then we put on Christmas music and gather around the tree to open gifts—one at a time. Christmas dinner comes late in the afternoon and is shared with cousins—our closest relatives in Indiana.
— *Marlene and Stanley Kropf, Elkhart, IN*

★ On Christmas Day, we used to have roast beef with Yorkshire pudding, until people stopped eating red meat. Now we have Cornish hens.
— *Joyce G. Zuercher, Hesston, KS*

★ We relax! We take a walk to the nearby woods or the lake if possible and enjoy a quiet day.
— *John and Joyce M. Petro, Kalamazoo, MI*

★ The dessert for our Christmas dinner is *always* a birthday cake for Jesus, complete with lighted candles. The youngest person present gets to blow out the candles after we sing "Happy Birthday" to Jesus.
— *Ruth Heatwole, Charlottesville, VA*

★ Our children prefer having Christmas Day at home with just our immediate family. We have a special Christmas meal with candles burning and a red tablecloth. It's not an elaborate meal, however. We always like to watch *A Christmas Carol*, often on Christmas Eve or Day.
— *Carl and Erma Horning, Lebanon, PA*

★ We always attend a church service in the morning. The children and grandchildren come home for lunch and supper. We sometimes go tobogganing in the afternoon, play games, sing, or just have naps. We open presents after supper.
— *Eleanor Kathler, Steinbach, Manitoba*

★ Sometime during the Christmas season, we try to tape each child. They put on tape whatever they want—songs, etc. Before taping, we listen to the previous years' recording. With five children, we learned too late that we should have put each child on a separate tape. It became a project later, making a tape for each child to keep.

— *James and Marian Payne, Heathsville, VA*

★ Christmas Day begins in a relaxed way. Neither our children nor grandchildren have insisted on an early rising. Frequently the grandchildren spend the night with us. In the morning when they are all awake, they open their stockings and discover fruit and nuts and trinkets. Then we have a leisurely breakfast with holiday breads, pastries, fruit, and special coffee for those who wish it.

Later, everyone helps with the dinner. We prepare a large pot of soup, homemade breads, green salad, and cinnamon apples filled with cream cheese. My mom always made these with the help of her granddaughters, and now I do it with my daughter and nieces who are around.

For dessert we have a layered trifle with strawberries, cake, and jello in the bottom; vanilla pudding with blueberries and bananas in the middle; and whipped cream on top with sliced chocolate.

— *Mary Ellen and Albert Meyer, Goshen, IN*

★ A friend of ours lets her children begin several days before Christmas to open one gift a day. Each gift is thoroughly enjoyed. Then Christmas day isn't so rushed.

— *Ben and Eunice Stoner, Farmington, NM*

*"The whole family also likes to wear red—
especially red sweat shirts—
on Christmas Day or at the gift exchange."*

★ We have Christmas dinner in the evening. We set the table with a bright red tablecloth.
— *Sara Zimmerly Ryan, Columbus, OH*

★ My oldest son, who works with a church in Bogota, Colombia, wrote a reading about the Christmas experience of many poor Colombians. The reading was about a family which we have come to know through my son's letters. All of our family members had a part in this reading. It was especially meaningful.
— *Carolyn Albrecht, Lancaster, PA*

★ We read the scripture before the gift exchange, but afterward we have a special Christmas story. Sometimes it is a children's book, storytelling, or a drama. The whole family also likes to wear red—especially red sweat shirts—on Christmas Day or at the gift exchange.
— *Eileen and Freeman Lehman, Kidron, OH*

9.
Additional Ideas and Traditions for Extended Families

★ We found a good intergenerational activity one year. Our extended family of 25 divided into groups. Using only newspapers, tape, and string, each group constructed a life-size part of the nativity scene. When Joseph, Mary, Jesus, the manger, wise men, shepherds, sheep, and cows were completed, we set them in place at one end of a large room. Then we gathered around the manger with them and sang Christmas songs.

—Steve and Phyllis Swartz, London, OH

★ We've been married 25 years, and I have a photo album of our Christmases each year. They include a picture of each family member (the number is growing), a short account of where we spent the holidays, what we did, and the main present each child got that year. I put the albums on the craft table each Christmas, and they get looked at many times.

—Jon and Esther Bucher, Marinville, Alberta

★ This year, in lieu of giving gifts, each person in our extended family brought an inexpensive gift. We auctioned these gifts at no more than $5 each. Then we sent the proceeds to a scholarship fund.

—James and Marian Payne, Heathsville, VA

★ During several recent years, after our dinner and gift opening, our family has gone to the community gym, which we rent for two hours of volleyball and other activities. Some people walk or play with the little ones on the sidelines. Playing together builds family memories and is an outlet for pent-up energy. Afterwards we return to the house for sandwiches and snacks.

—Walter and Lorene Good, Armington, IL

★ When the Weber extended family gathers for the day, one person is responsible for painting a simple mural scene. In the course of the day, everyone present paints themselves into the picture. The murals are saved and provide an amusing portrait of the family at different stages.

— *Ann and Byron Weber Becker, Kitchener, Onatrio*

> *"Each New Year's Day,*
> *each of the 10 children*
> *brings memories to tell*
> *during a sharing time."*

★ Several years ago, a new tradition was started by my mother's family. She comes from a farming family of five sons and five daughters. You can imagine all the experiences and memories accumulated during their growing up years!

Each New Year's Day when the entire family is together, each of the 10 children is asked to bring along memories and stories from their childhoods, to tell during a sharing time. It is a warm and hilarious time, as well as revealing! I value these times as opportunities to learn about my family and to be thankful.

— *Melanie Gochnauer, Columbia, PA*

★ For 15 years, we lived many miles from any extended family, but Janet's mother always spent two weeks visiting us during the Christmas season. She came in time to take in the girls' Christmas programs at school and church and stayed until New Year's. One of our favorite activities with Grandma was our after-Christmas shopping spree! We went to a mall three or four days after Christmas to see what we could find on sale!

— *Janet, Larry, Susan, and Kara Dixon, Topeka, KS*

★ We travel to one family at Thanksgiving, and to the other either before Thanksgiving or after Epiphany. We intentionally don't travel in between because it makes an otherwise special month, too hectic.

—Cindy Bryant Weidman, Richmond, VA

★ Anybody attending the clan Christmas for the first time is honored by a hand-carved hazelnut yo-yo, a tradition that goes back at least 50 years in the Juhnke family.

—James and Anna Juhnke, North Newton, KS

★ I, Margaret, grew up in Ethiopia, Africa, as a missionary kid. Our family all learned to love the Ethiopian food, injera and wat, a very spicy stew eaten with a thin pancake-like bread.

Now as we eight children return to the homeplace in Pennsylvania for Christmas each year (some of us with our own children), our big meal of the season is injera and wat (see the recipes on pages 32 and 33.) And do we ever eat! We enjoy not only the wonderful flavors, but also the childhood memories.

—Margaret, Samuel, Bart, and Hannah
Wenger Johnson, Keezletown, VA

> *"Some of the younger children*
> *think "Illinois" is a motel*
> *with a swimming pool where they*
> *spend time with cousins from Iowa!*

★ After our extended family has had a traditional meal, we open presents that we exchange by drawing names. Then we always attempt to sing portions of *The Messiah!* At one time or another we have all been in a church choir or college choir which has performed it, so the music is very familiar and we enjoy trying to sing it.

—Elaine Lepp Karber, Long Beach, CA

★ Every other year, our extended family meets at a camp. We rent one building lodge with cooking and sleeping facilities. The families come from California to Vermont with almost 100% participation. We are together for about three days with food, games (indoor and outdoor), gift exchange, and church services. Those age 50 and over go home for the night; most of the rest sleep together in one big room. As great-grandchildren are added, sleeping rooms are added. We share cooking and clean-up responsibilities. We plan menus and shop ahead of time. All 32 of us look forward to this with eagerness.

— Curt and Gloria Nussbaum, Kidron, OH

★ Our extended family usually meets on New Year's Day for a meal and to watch sports. We plan a menu, and each family supplies a part of the dinner. We stretch out tables to accommodate everyone from the youngest to the oldest.

In the evening we make "Knee Patches" or "Nothings." They were a popular treat at Swiss weddings and holiday feasts.

— John and Trula Zimmerly, Jackson, OH

Knee Patches

3 eggs   **4 cups flour**
1 cup cream   **½ tsp. salt**

1. Beat the eggs well. Stir in cream.
2. Sift dry ingredients. Mix with wet ingredients to make a soft dough.
3. Pinch off a piece of dough the size of a marble. Roll it out and stretch it to make it very thin.
4. Fry in deep fat at 375° until delicately brown.
5. Drain and dust with powdered sugar.
6. Repeat until dough is all gone.

★ We and most of our adult children live in Indiana, while most of our relatives live in Iowa. So my side of the family meets each year, the weekend before Thanksgiving, at a motel in Illinois about halfway between our homes. There are four generations of us, and it is a special time for each age group. Some of the younger children think "Illinois" is a motel with a swimming pool where they spend time with cousins from Iowa!

—Dan and Annabelle Unternahrer, Shipshewana, IN

★ My parents inherited a big iron that makes "New Year's Cakes." You put a very thin dough into the iron, and then hold it over the stove. It takes about one minute to do one cake. Then another person needs to be ready to quickly roll the cake on a wooden stick. It tastes like a thin ice cream cone. It is fun to work together with children, parents, and grandparents to accomplish this after the Christmas holidays.

—Joyce Eigsti Hofer, Denver, CO

★ Ray's family is scattered—some in Pennsylvania and some in British Columbia. Last Christmas Ray's mom and dad were not looking forward to a Christmas alone. Our kids wanted to be with Grandma and Grandpa for Christmas, but it didn't seem possible. Ray entered a contest ("Bring your loved ones home for Christmas"), and won a trip for two by train for his parents. They came to spend Christmas with us, all expenses paid—a real miracle! We had a wonderful time all together. The kids just loved having Grandma and Grandpa here for Christmas.

— Ray, Katie, Lauren, and Alexa Dirks
Winnipeg, Manitoba

★ My father was born on Christmas day. As my grandmother used to tell it, "Friends would say, 'What a pity to be born on Christmas day; he will never be able to celebrate his birthday properly.'" But she was determined that he would never regret having the same birthday as Jesus, so they had a birthday celebration for Jesus in the morning, and in the afternoon his friends would come to a birthday party for my father, complete with cake and ice cream. "He received double presents that day."

— David and Louisa Mow, Farmington, PA

★ A number of my family members gather to help at my brother and sister-in-law's farm during the days right before Christmas, which is the busiest season for them. It is often a lively occasion, and we enjoy the chance to spend time together while we work. During the vacation, there is no shortage of the product we've worked on—*celery!*

—*Elaine Shenk, Elkhart, IN*

★ In 1988 my brothers and sisters and I decided to write a book about our growing-up years. Each of us wrote a story about our memories from childhood, up to our marriages. We each titled our own stories. Then we added stories about our parents, grandparents, and great-grandparents, plus family pictures. We put it all together into a book, with a picture on the center painted by my sister of our childhood home. Each of the grandchildren received one of those books that Christmas. This project took a year to complete, from January until December. We still have lots of books left for our great-grandchildren.

—*Marjora Miller, Archbold, OH*

★ When I was growing up, my grandparents always had foreign students in their home. Christmas always included our family, plus a number of foreigners. I grew up rarely leaving Lancaster County, yet knowing people from all over the world.

—*Dawn J. Ranck, Strasburg, PA*

★ When our family members come with their friends to visit at Christmas, we often tour historical sites and museums. This opens the doors to remembering our immigrant family histories, storytelling, evaluating, and it goes on and on. Holiday seasons are wonderful times for communicating with and about family!

—*Cornelia and Arlie J. Regier, Overland Park, KS*

★ For as long as I can remember, my mother's family (grandparents, children, and grandchildren—my generation) drew names and exchanged gifts at Christmas. Recently, however, as we grandchildren have grown up and gotten married, the extended family has grown more distant, and choosing gifts has become a chore. In an effort to maintain our connections to each other, we've decided to transform the exchange from one of "gifts" to one of "contact" (a phone call, a letter, or the like). Now we can restore what's most important—our relationships.

— *Suzanne Marie Hitt, Fairfield, OH*

★ We live far away from all extended family, so we seldom ever see any of them. Since my husband and I both grew up with the tradition of doing jigsaw puzzles at Christmas-time, we still set up the table and do several 1000-piece puzzles during the Christmas holidays. Everyone who is around participates; even guests add pieces since the table is set up where everyone has clear access.

— *Norma J. Pauls, Oakville, Ontario*

> *"The tradition has become
> to have no tradition
> when it comes to
> Christmas dinner."*

★ Our son's wife is of Italian background and always had lasagna on Christmas day. We decided this was a good practice, so we have begun to do the same.
— *Carl Jantzen, Seven Mile, OH*

★ With my family, we try new dishes every year—the tradition has become to have no tradition when it comes to Christmas dinner.
— *Dorcas Breckbill, Newmanstown, PA*

★ During the holidays we always have Sisters Day. My sisters and I go to a play, museum, movie, tourist spot, or shopping trip—or just spend the day together without children. Sometimes we invite Mom to go, too. These days are always fun, renewing and memorable.
— *Laura and Steve Blosser Draper, Winfield, IA*

★ When our children were little, Grandma made them each a "12 days of Christmas" package. It had 12 gifts, to be opened each day after Christmas. The children really enjoyed the small goodies that extended the holiday celebration.
— *Heidi Eash, Bristol, IN*

★ In both of our extended families, we rent local school gyms for a Christmas afternoon get-together of rousing games of basketball, volleyball, indoor soccer, four-square, hockey, prisoners base, or steal-the-bacon.
— *Jewel Showalter, Landisville, PA*

> *"If gifts become too big*
> *for the stocking*
> *we create*
> *a stocking to size.*
> *(We've had some*
> *wonderfully creative stockings.)"*

★ In my family of five siblings, we always played our musical instruments following our gift exchange. My father played a Hawaiian guitar, my brother and I played guitars, my oldest sister an accordion, and two other sisters played ukuleles. Our music wasn't too great, but we had great fun.

—*Jane Hoober Peifer, Harrisonburg, VA*

★ We gather for an hour or two after the meal to sing hymns and choral numbers and family favorites. Everyone from about age 10 and above participates. One year we made a tape recording of our Christmas songfest.

—*Marlene and Stanley Kropf, Elkhart, IN*

★ Instead of exchanging gifts, our extended family (uncles, aunts, cousins) gather yearly near Christmas at a camp for a meal, overnight, and breakfast. The children look forward to staying up late that night to play with cousins. Adults play table games, talk, or sing.

There's usually someone who has traveled during the past year or has some other special event to share with the whole group. No one has to cook because meals are cooked by the camp staff, but we do bring snacks. This tradition has become very important to our family and is one that the children look forward to, year after year, as much as receiving gifts.

—*Leona Kraybill Myer, Pittsburgh, PA*

★ We cut the whole Christmas story into 15 parts and used those pieces in a treasure hunt. We drew a map and put a star at each location where the teams could find a part of the story. After the teams had all collected all their Christmas story pieces, they came back to the barn and put all the story parts in order. We read the Christmas story together, and then celebrated with a piñata made by several of the cousins.

—Helen Stoltzfus Bowman, Millersburg, IN

★ Instead of doing a lot of shopping, we take our extended family—children and grandchildren—on a ski weekend the weekend before Christmas. There are 13 of us.

We choose names each year for the next Christmas and each stuffs one stocking for the name each pulls. If gifts become too big for the stocking, we create a stocking to size. (We've had some wonderfully creative stockings.) We encourage creative gifts, and have a year to think about this—also our name becomes a secret prayer partner for the year. Our children would not miss this event for anything. And it's great to be together without distractions.

—Hildegarde Baerg, Abbotsford, British Columbia

★ On alternate years, we are usually with Willard's family in Iowa. Along with a holiday meal together, we observe the tradition of Psalm Bag (which came from Germany two generations back). In a cloth bag—in olden days a salt sack—are small card squares with numbers from 1-150. Beginning with the oldest family member, each picks a number and then reads the appropriate Psalm around the family circle.

—Alice and Willard Roth, Elkhart, IN

★ After Christmas I enjoy making scrapbooks. I include favorite cards, napkins, photos, illustrations from Christmas catalogues, and grandchildren's Christmas programs.

—Dale and Rosie Horst, Newton, KS

10.

Keeping the Spirit of Christmas Alive

★ I try to remind myself regularly that when my children are older and more independent, I will have the time and energy to do some of the things that now go undone. Rather than lament the programs that are interrupted, I try to remember that in the future our children will have the ability to sit through special Christmas programs.

Rather than spend my time wishing they would grow up

quickly, I want to make our Christmas something that my daughters will enjoy and that will include activities appropriate for their age. A friend of mine talks of "making memories" during summer vacation months, and I try to bring that mode of thought to our family Christmas celebration.

This year we hosted one social event in our home during the holidays: my daughter and I planned a Mother/Daughter Christmas Tea for two preschool friends and their moms. Our menu was simple (no stress), each of us held a toddler on our laps (high stress!), and the girls did more playing than eating. But it was something Amanda and I planned together and something she enjoyed.

— Connie Faber, Hillsboro, KS

> ## "The stable door folds up and becomes a carrying case which the children take all over with them so they can play 'Baby Jesus' wherever they want to."

★ We have three manger scenes. One stays on a shelf where everyone can see it but not touch it. Another is under the Christmas tree and gets rearranged on a regular basis. The third is made of fabric, and the figures are like little stuffed pillows. The stable door folds up and becomes a carrying case which the children take all over with them so they can play "Baby Jesus" wherever they want to.

Our congregation always has a mitten tree, where everyone is invited to hang a pair of mittens on a tree in the lobby. After Christmas, they are given to one of the city's homeless shelters to distribute.

— John and Sandra Drescher-Lehman, Richmond, VA

> ## *"We don't use credit cards throughout the month of December."*

★ One year my husband had several Thai students in his class. In talking with one of them, he found out she was a good cook and missed having a kitchen to do her cooking. She was eager to cook a meal for us. The day before Christmas she and I went shopping to pick up the things she needed that we did not have on hand.

The next day, Norashita and several friends came to our home. I showed them where things were in the kitchen and turned it over to them. I retired to the family room to play games with the children. That day we had a delicious Thai meal with four or five foreign students. The thing our children enjoyed the most was that they could eat with their fingers. In typical Thai style, we had no utensils on the table.

— Grace and Werner Will, Stevensville, MT

★ For reasons of economy and ecology, our family has for many years had great early Christmas Eve adventures, searching for a *free* Christmas tree. All season long we watch for unfenced Christmas tree lots. When they are finally abandoned on Christmas Eve, often with an assortment of nice unsold trees, we pick out one—sometimes three or four—and take them home.

We set up a larger tree by the entrance and forthwith decorate it with silver icicles and the family collection of homemade and painted ornaments. Sometimes when we have several smaller trees, we theme-decorate (all angels, all musical instruments, or all hand-painted ornaments made by the children), and place them in the bedrooms and dining room as well.

— Dawn Pichette, Harbor City, CA

★ We find that keeping a sense of humor when our gift budget is quite restricted helps.
                    —*Janet, Larry, Susan, and Karen Dixon, Topeka, KS*

★ I take time to write notes on all the cards we send. I like to keep up with friends around the country. And I send cards only to the people I won't be able to see. Some people don't like form letters, but I don't mind. It is really the only way to keep up with widely scattered friends.
                    —*Sarah Yoder Scott, Newark, DE*

★ We prepare for this occasion all year-round. We also believe that Christmas is an occasion to welcome the strangers, the weary, the less-fortunate, the hungry. Persons from other countries who have experienced Christmas in the Philippines say that we are the "eat wonder of the world."
                    —*Luis A. Lumibao, San Jose City, Philippines*

★ The following idea was begun years ago by my mother, and we have done it, too. Children and grandchildren choose items (keepsakes) culled from our shelves and drawers—games, books, dishes, tools, etc. I usually buy a few new items so that the choice includes something practical for those who are not so sentimental or interested in items with a history.
                    —*LaVerna Klippenstein, Winnipeg, Manitoba*

★ The first Christmas after our 20-year-old son was killed, we would have wished to stop Christmas and all its traditions because the memories were so painful. But traditions give continuity and meaning, and extended families wanted to gather, so we have not changed traditions.
                    —*Curt and Gloria Nussbaum, Kidron, OH*

★ We don't use credit cards throughout the month of December. The result is that we don't spend money we don't have.

We use a wooden Advent calendar. Each morning the children eagerly open a small basket which contains that day's wooden figure, to be added to the nativity scene on the wooden board that serves as the Advent calendar. The children enjoy finding a new piece every day and adding it to the calendar. This keeps the story of Jesus' birth unfolding before our eyes throughout the month in a colorful way.

— *Gwen Gustafson-Zook, Portland, OR*

"That paper is mounted on the ceiling all year long."

★ We try to have a week in December called "soup week." Each evening we have soup and bread for our evening meal. Our family then sends a money gift to overseas relief. It is a small attempt to "feel" some of the world's need.

— *David and Martha Clymer family Shirleysburg, PA*

★ During the busy Christmas season, I am often reminded of Doris Longacre's statement: "Life is too short to get ready for Christmas; just let Christmas come." That has helped me put things into proper perspective many times.

— *Gloria Lehman, Singers Glen, VA*

★ The year we bought our farm, we told the children that they would only receive one small gift. It had no effect at all on the excitement and "specialness" of Christmas. When a schoolmate remarked that our son's gift "isn't very much," he replied, "Oh, but we're getting a farm!"

— *Norman and Ruth Smith, Ailsa Craig, Ontario*

★ Our family calendar includes three birthdays in December and January, so it often feels like we celebrate non-stop from Thanksgiving until mid-January. I try to eliminate all extra activities and say no to many interesting ones during this time, in order to protect family time. We try to focus on time together with friends and family rather than on gifts.

—Rod and Martha Yoder Maust, Indianapolis, IN

★ We have learned to drop traditions that are a lower priority for us. At one time we made peppernuts as a family, but now we simply *remember* the fun of cutting and baking all those tiny little morsels. At one time we had a Jesse Tree, with symbols and scriptures from Adam and Eve to Joseph and Mary, to mark each day in December. Now we are too busy to enjoy it, so we let it go.

—Jim, Lois, Britt, Austin, Reid, and Lane Kaufmann
New Paris, IN

★ We have learned not to make December 25 a deadline. The entire month of December includes celebration and preparation; we also let our activities flow into the new year. Our son-in-law says, "Slow down and savor the flavor of the season."

—Alvin and Edna Mast, Manheim, PA

★ On Thanksgiving Day (which is kind of the opener for Christmas), we take a long piece of paper (newsprint or something like it), and we all contribute by writing or drawing persons and things for which we're thankful. That paper is mounted on the ceiling all year long.
  — *Ben and Eunice Stoner, Farmington, NM*

★ As our children have grown older, we do less baking and try instead to have more fresh fruit on hand like grapes, kiwi, tangerines. We always have a big wooden bowl of nuts in the shell and sit around cracking and eating after meals. We enjoy hot drinks like wassail, mulled cider, and friendship tea.
  — *Jewel Showalter, Landisville, PA*

★ After my mother died three years ago at Christmas-time, I didn't feel like celebrating Christmas for a few years. But now I light the candles for her and feel her joy of the season coming through again. (She loved Christmas.)
  — *Jane Brubaker, Leaburg, OR*

★ Our senior Sunday school class has a Christmas covered dish dinner. We exchange gifts, play games, and sing carols. The meal ticket is a can of food to be given to our local food bank.
  — *Erma Kauffman, Cochranville, PA*

★ I start early to collect dried flowers and to find ideas to make many gifts for friends and family—usually at a very low cost. Starting early keeps away the pressure and increases the enjoyment.
  — *Jon and Esther Bucher, Marinville, Alberta*

★ I find using Advent candles a very good centering device to calm me in the face of all the activity and refocus me on what is important.
  — *Joe and Laura Bare, New Braunfels, TX*

★   Our formula for modest spending is not exciting, but it works—we save a designated amount of money each month throughout the year, and then decide how to divide it up when the season comes.

— *Marlene and Stanley Kropf, Elkhart, IN*

★   One year we shared our Christmas with a very depressed older student of mine who had returned to college and was experiencing a divorce. She later said we saved her from suicide. After 25 years, we still hear from her at Christmas.

— *James and Marian Payne, Heathsville, VA*

★   We try always to keep before us—by talking about it, but also by practicing it during the year—that the good news of Christ and the giving nature of God help us give appropriately to those we love. We teach that giving can be enriched for both giver and receiver when we carefully consider the values, dreams, needs, and character of the recipient by the gifts we choose and the ways we give them.

— *Clare and Ben Neufeld, Delta, British Columbia*

★   I've heard about a tradition for Thanksgiving, but it could also be used for Christmas. Throughout the year, fill a jar with

slips of paper containing various answers to prayers. At Christmas-time, open the jar and read all the blessings God provided that year!

—*Kay Driver, Columbus, OH*

★ Creating decorations from items you collect from nature helps one to appreciate and enjoy the preparations more. It also is very economical and amazing how much you can do without spending much money. The time you spend is precious and meaningful, especially if family members can work together at creating decorations.

—*Norma J. Pauls, Oakville, Ontario*

> *"One year when Mother was sick and the children were small, our church brought gifts and stockings."*

★ We no longer buy wrapping paper but use homemade cloth bags. We recycle cards and gift tags. We use less sugar in Christmas baking. We eat less candy and more fresh fruit. We go out less. We have friends over for meals and donate money to a local food bank.

—*Jake and Herta Janzen, Coledale, Alberta*

★ One year when Mother was sick and the children were small, our church brought gifts and stockings. That stands out in our memory as a wonderful time because of our church friends' involvement and generosity.

—*Ben and Lorraine Myers, Dillsburg, PA*

★ Our family guideline on decorating, music, and baking: "If it's more burden than fun, don't do it!"

—*Caprice Becker and Richard Harris, Manhattan, KS*

> ## *"We decided that a tree branch painted gold would be our new Christmas tree."*

★ We don't feel obligated to send Christmas cards in December. We often send them in January instead.
> —*Karen Miller Rush, Harrisonburg, VA*

★ We are always aware of the uniqueness of Christmas and we want to keep the spirit free and joyful and thankful. Sometimes we have to consciously cut down on activities, and on buying and giving, so that we can enjoy the true meaning of Christmas.

We always had a big green, living, pine-smelling, Christmas tree, but when we moved to a townhouse, we decided that a tree branch painted gold would be our new Christmas tree. We saved the small ornaments from our big tree and used those to decorate. It is much easier, takes less time and energy to trim, and saves on space when space is at a premium.
> —*Joyce Eigsti Hofer, Denver, CO*

★ We have decided to invite someone who will be alone at Christmas to join our family for one evening of our Christmas celebration.
> —*Walter J. Quiring, Calgary, Alberta*

★ We make time during December to help sort the donated canned/boxed foods that come to the Salvation Army and to pack food boxes and toy bags for needy families. It's something we all can do. (Our children are ages six and eight.)

When we were making a list of things to do over Christmas vacation this year, I asked Stevie if he wanted to add anything. He gave me two items, one of which was "to help at the Salvation Army."
> —*Matthew, Barbara, Stephen, and Naomi Woolsey*
> *Batavia, NY*

> ## *"I enjoyed it so much
> I've thought of volunteering
> to work Christmas Eve
> next year!*

★ I write a Christmas letter, giving a sketch of family news throughout the year. I've done this since our children were small, so the collection of letters now provides a chronology of our family's history. At one point, I made each of our four children a book containing the letters and the pictures of them we sent at Christmas through the years.
— *Jeanette Ediger Flaming, Dallas, OR*

★ My husband, Galen, has prepared up to 120 luminaries for our Christmas church services, either for the night of the Christmas program or the Christmas Eve service. He uses gallon milk jugs with sand and any partially burned candles he can salvage. Many people have commented about how much they appreciate these glowing lights around our rural church—letting our lights shine!
— *Gloria Lehman, Singers Glen, VA*

★ One year when our children were small, chipmunks got into a basket of hickory nuts which we had gathered in our backyard to shell later. They chewed each one of the nuts in the same way, so we strung the nuts and shellacked them for necklaces for the grandparents in Pennsylvania and Ontario.
— *James and Helen Reusser, Kitchener, Ontario*

★ One year all of the churches in our community gathered in the renovated and restored historic church in Hillsboro for a pre-Christmas celebration with singing, readings, drama. The church, more than 100 years old, is a gem and lends itself well for gatherings which don't require cathedral-sized space. The warmth of community togetherness enveloped the capacity crowd. It was a very special community coming-together to celebrate the birth of our Savior.

—*Frank and Marie Wiens, Hillsboro, KS*

★ This past Christmas Eve I was feeling sad as I prepared to work the 3-11 shift as an R.N. on a psychiatric unit, because I was unable to attend the Christmas Eve service at church. Then the thought came to me, "If I can't attend the Christmas Eve service, I can take it to my patients who also cannot attend."

I planned a service of carols and readings. Patients willingly read the scriptures. A young college music major sang, "O Holy Night." I accompanied the carols on the piano. A short reading spoke of experiencing the meaning of Christmas away from home. Afterwards, many patients expressed appreciation for the service. I enjoyed it so much I've thought of volunteering to work Christmas Eve next year!

—*Leona Kraybill Myer, Pittsburgh, PA*

About the Authors

Phyllis Pellman Good and Merle Good have teamed together on a variety of projects, beginning in the early '70s with an experimental theater.

Today they jointly oversee the operation of a small publishing house and a collection of galleries and museums in Intercourse, Pennsylvania, a village in eastern Lancaster County.

The Goods have each authored numerous books. They also collaborated on an earlier book which serves as a companion to this one entitled *Ideas for Families*.

The Goods are parents of two teenage daughters and live in the city of Lancaster.